The Black Girl on Prozac

Tales from the iPhone and a Look Inside an Anxious Mind

Andrea E. Paul

B.O.S.S. Publishing

The Black Girl on Prozac: Tales from the iPhone and a Look Inside an Anxious Mind

For information, contact,
B.O.S.S. Publishing
4820 Walden Lake Point
Decatur, GA 30035

For information regarding special discounts for bulk purchases, sales, promotions, speaking engagements and or book clubs, please contact us by email at: sales@boss-emag.com.

Manufactured in the United States of America

ISBN 978-0-9863559-6-7

10 9 8 7 6 5 4 3 2

Dedication

Thank you to the priceless friends and family who have held my hand, stayed up late with me, called to make sure I ate, listened to my confusing thoughts, and simply loved on me through this difficult time. Howard Clay, Myeeah Scott, Theresa Thomas, Angel Amos, and Allison Gravesande.

To my psychologist, Dr. Angela Bethea-Walsh for listening to me say "I don't know" week after week and for taking a risk on me. To my pychiatrist, Dr. Jennifer Wooten, thank you for trying to understand what I was experiencing and for working with me to find the right treatment for me.

Shoutout to Prozac (Fluoxetine) for allowing me to be able to write this. Without it, there would be no book!

Thank you to myself, for coming from a dark place and realizing that there is indeed light at the end of the tunnel. One of my best friends has this quote tattooed on her shoulder: "It is always darkest before dawn." Time to wake up the chickens!

Lastly, but definitely not least, thank you so much to the countless number of women- minority women especially- who decided to make a change for the better in their mental health life. Thank you for not being afraid to tell your story to a complete stranger in order to get the help you needed. Thank you for letting those of us coming after you know that it is okay to not be "fine" all the time.

Thank you. Thank you. Thank you.

To all of you, I am eternally endebted.

Introduction

What does it mean to have a mental illness? How does it feel to go from being the life of the party to Debbie Downer in the same day? How confused would you be if you had no idea what your mind was doing?

Hi. I'm Andrea and I am currently going through my own mental health journey. Through out this book, I put my feelings, thoughts, and emotions out there, in plain sight. My goal is to shed a light on the fact that anxiety and depression are very much present in the African-American community. It is only through cultural channels that we misinterpret a "sick brain" as being lazy, ungrateful, and "the devil." Of course, naturally, I asked, "why me?" The knee-jerk reaction I had to that was, "why not me?" I'm the best person to share my story, so I need a story to share.

Why can't we recognize the problems we face and seek the appropriate help?

I want everyone who reads this book to do so with an open mind. I want you to realize that someone close to you, right now (either in physical or emotional proximity), is suffering mentally. It could be anyone from your younger cousin to the guy who sat next to you on the train. If it happens to be you, I encourage you to reach out to a counselor, therapist, or even a trusting friend who you can openly speak to. Seek out proper resources in your area so that you can confidently know that you are taking steps in the right direction. For me, that initial resource was my University's counseling center. For you, it may be your city or county's behavioral health clinic or the teaching hospital. If it is someone you know, be willing to hear their story and to offer sound, nonjudgmental advice.

Don't see your need for help, treatment, therapy, or medication as a weakness. It definitely takes strength to understand and accept something is wrong and then to ask for assistance. Join me on my journey through anxiety, depression, and a new diagnoses while I had been taking the antidepressant, Prozac. It was definitely a roller coaster ride with unexpected twists and turns.

#AdventuresWithDrea

Introduction

Introduction

•••○○ Sprint LTE 8:59 PM

< **Notes**

June 25, 2015

Today was the first day. I took a well deserved trip to the neighborhood Waffle House to enjoy the inaugural day of the rest of my life. Taking a bit of my waffle, I prepared the little plastic green and white pill to enter my life. I threw it to the back of my throat and swallowed. I don't know what I felt... like I had given in to being crazy? Guilty? Relieved? No clue. I just know I had done it.

The day seemed to go on equally uneventfully. After devouring my meal, I went home and crashed. Mind you, it was 11am on a Thursday. When I woke up an hour and a half later, I felt as though I had been asleep for a hundred years. It was the most rested I had felt in a very long time. I got dressed and headed to a business meeting. No big deal. By now, I had forgotten I had taken the medication

••••∘ Sprint LTE

< Notes

a few hours earlier. I was still feeling normal, but I was restless. I wanted to walk around, possibly jump and run and climb the walls, but I couldn't put my finger on the feeling. Once that was over, I made my way home, drained from interacting with people, as is very normal for me. I changed out of my business clothes and laid in bed ready to call it a day at 4pm.

On a regular day, I would scroll through Instagram until I was falling asleep with my finger on the screen hoping I didn't accidentally like someone's picture. Today, that didn't happen. I was beyond sleepy and more than ready to end the day, but my body just wouldn't let me. It was wide awake, but I was tired... I was yawning every 5 minutes and forcing my eyes shut, only to find myself staring at the ceiling fan that did nothing to cool my

•••oo Sprint LTE

< Notes

room.

3 hours later, here I am, still staring at the fan and writing this. I seem to be noticing every little thing happening to my body right now. I have a headache that is worse on the right side of my forehead and when I blink, I feel the pain in my face. My stomach hurts. I don't feel sick or nauseous, it literally hurts. My abs twitch... more so the left side. My intestines are churning. My toes are tense. Am I nervous? My jaw is tense. My shoulders are tense. My heart seems to want out of its pericardial space in my chest. It's beating so hard right now... not fast, but just hard. My breathing is irregular. At this moment it is like I hold my breath for a while longer than normal before I exhale again.

•••○○ Sprint LTE

< Notes

There is more, but if I decide to list them, it would be tedious.

My mind is nowhere, yet it is everywhere. I'm not thinking of anything. Almost like a blank canvas. Something's there, but again, I can't put my finger on it.

Intrusive thoughts suck. Today I've wondered about choking my cat, throwing a glass down the stairs of my house and just leaving it there for someone to step in, ramming my car into the front of the house, and throwing myself down the steps.

Yeah. Big fun.

...Bright side.

I spoke to people today. That's a win, no?

•••oo Sprint LTE 9:45 AM

< Notes

June 28, 2015

Up until this point everything has been very anticlimactic. My "side effects" are still the same, so I've come to appreciate them as "the new normal." But, I woke up today and something is drastically different.

No. I haven't taken my meds yet today.

The thing is, I don't want to.

When I opened my eyes this morning, the sun was shining so bright into my room, my cat was asleep next to me on the bed, and the breeze from the ceiling fan blew over me ever so lightly. Everything was very quiet and very still. I just laid there, staring at the ceiling. I had no thoughts running through my mind- at least no conscious thought. I didn't want to move which was strange for me. Whenever I

●●●○○ Sprint LTE

< Notes

wake up, my first instinct is to pick up my phone and see the night's happenings on Instagram. I didn't want to do that today.

I just laid there.

I guess it was kind of serene, but that's what freaked me out. This was strange. This was uncomfortable. I didn't like it. I didn't understand it. Any normal person would bask in feeling the warmth from the sun on their face as they awakened ever so gently from their deep slumber. Nope. Not I.

I don't like this, not one bit. I know that this (taking medicine) is a step in the right direction to getting better, but I don't want it. I don't feel safe. I don't feel comfort. I feel as though I am being pushed off the edge of a cliff in slow motion. This isn't

•••oo Sprint LTE

< **Notes**

ME. I am not this person I am becoming.

But I digress.

It is almost time for my reminder alarm to go off. We'll see if I remain a compliant patient or if I decide to remain the person I am comfortable being. We'll soon find out.

•••oo Sprint LTE 10:35 AM

< Notes

July 5, 2015

I haven't stopped. I've been a good, compliant patient and have been taking my pills on time, everyday. I know things need to change and I have accepted that. I just need to keep up with it despite the migraines, the muscle aches, and impromptu moments of zoning out. It will all be worth it in the end, right?

I understand that this is a change I need to embrace, a change that is for the better, but why does it have to feel so... drastic? I am not the same person I was 2 weeks ago and that scares me. How could it all be shifting so fast?

Just living life, I know that change is envitable (unless youre one of those people who choose to remain stagnant their entire lives). But, is this change I am

●●●○○ Sprint LTE

< **Notes**

experiencing worth it? Are the side effects worth it?

Is my sanity worth it?

I guess I think highly of myself to want to get help. Yes. I am worth it. It's just something I need to embrace and get it over with.

Le sigh.

I'm worth it. Aren't I?

•••○○ Sprint LTE 10:56 AM

< Notes

July 7, 2015

I went to see my psychologist yesterday. Thanks to my school's *awesome* shuttle service, I was late for my appointment and it freaked me out. When I got into her office, I apologized so much... you would have thought I ran over her childhood pet with my car. I felt so bad and it showed. All that for being 3 minutes late.

After that initial shock, the session went on. We addressed my OCD tendencies when it comes to my life. I've always known (and said) that I need everything to be clear cut. I need for everything to be either A or B... there must be definitive answers and everything must fit neatly in its own perfect little boxes. I explained that I understood clearly that life will give me square pegs and round holes, but that I just cannot operate with ambiguity. She

•••○○ Sprint LTE

< Notes

quickly told me that for things that cannot fit in a perfect place, I have to learn to redefine its meaning and create a new place for said things to fit. Seems easy enough.

I think I like her. Maybe because if I had continued in the psychology major in undergrad, I would be her. She definitely reminds me of myself... or at least makes me wonder "what if."

I haven't taken my medication yet today. I'm about an hour late. I feel really guilty about that, but I'm cramping really bad. (Hello Mother Nature!) I just don't want to move from my bed yet. I plan to take it whenever I get up. Hopefully, I don't forget.

Other than the pain and slight guilt, I feel

●●●○○ Sprint LTE

< Notes

like I'm having an "up" day. Hopefully, it stays that way.

Prozac- 1

Me - 10

•••oo Sprint LTE 5:40 AM

< **Notes**

July 8, 2015

Why am I wide awake?! I've been up for an hour now and I don't understand why. I feel like I could go run a marathon right now with how alert I am. All this coming from the girl who won't leave her bed most days...

I go see my psychiatrist for my first follow up visit today. Is this significant enough to tell her about? I mean, I had a really good day yesterday.

A REALLY GOOD DAY.

And now I'm sitting here thinking it was a fluke. Here I go with my catastrophic thinking... I did drink mass green tea yesterday. I was cramping... I needed something. So, maybe it's that? But, I went to bed after 10pm. That means I shouldn't wake up TIL around 10am. 7 if

•••oo Sprint LTE 10:56 AM

< Notes

July 7, 2015

my cat wakes me.

I'm so wired right now. My mind is racing everywhere. Do I have ADD now? Yeah, it's that bad right now. Usually, I think of nothing and my mind is simply floating in a black abyss or I'm thinking about how messed up my life is, so for me to be thinking and feeling how I am is beyond strange and I don't know how to handle it.

Maybe the meds are working?

I spoke to my best friend yesterday. She knows about my situation and I jokingly told her, "don't I sound like the Prozac is kicking in?" In my jovial, happy, yet sarcastic voice. She tried to play me and said that it takes 4-6 weeks for it to start working. She would know. She's a doctor. That kinda negated my optimism (where

•••oo Sprint LTE 8:56 PM

< Notes

June 15, 2015

has THAT been?) for this treatment to be working. I mean, placebo effect is real.

I'll tell the psychiatrist today and see what she says.

I don't know where my mind will continue to take me while I lie here awake. Hopefully, it will stop soon.

•••○○ Sprint LTE 10:10 AM

< **Notes**

July 10, 2015

Nope.

I can't today. It's only 10 and I am already over the day. I've already eaten and have taken my medicine. I just want to sleep and cry.

When I went to see my psychiatrist on Wednesday, she was surprised at the progress I made. Tuesday was an amazing day. Wednesday wasn't as great, but it was good. Yesterday was *meh*, and today is already crappy. I don't understand. I thought things were supposed to be going upwards, not bouncing around like a beach ball.

The fact that my friends keep calling to talk on the phone is irking me so bad. Like, we've NEVER talked on the phone. Either we spoke in person or texted. I

••••○ Sprint LTE

< Notes

don't like the phone. Please stop calling me! Don't get me started on FaceTime! Hate it. Stop calling me.

I love you but stop calling me, please.

Ugh. I wish the day was over.

●●●○○ Sprint LTE 11:26M

< Notes

JULY 10, 2015

Text to my best friend:

I think I'm having a break down or crisis or something. Like I feel super ridiculously anxious. I can't sit still. I feel out of breath and like my heart is beating hard- not fast. I want to cry and scream and run around like I just ate a jar of sugar. But I feel tired. Fatigued is a better word. I don't know what to do. I'm not thinking of anything specific so no true identifiable trigger. I want to punch the wall and sleep. I took my pill at 9. Idk what to do. It kinda freaking me out but I feel like I'll be okay. But idk. Just thought I'd tell someone. Not looking for a reply.

I've always had anxious moments. But, now that I have a word and definition for it, I think Im abusing it. Before, when anxiety would creep up on me, I took it as a 6th

•••○○ Sprint LTE

< Notes

sense... something was wrong with someone I was close to. I would call my friends and ask, " is everything okay?" and they would almost always reply that something was wrong with them. It was my *gut feeling*. Once they confirmed that for me, life went on, as per normal.

Now, things are spiraling out of control and I feel like I'm being selfish because now, everything is actually all about me. My mind is racing and I can't make it stop. I just want to be normal and not freak out because now, I know I can because I have an actual diagnosis. I'm being selfish. I really am and I need to get over it.

•••○○ Sprint LTE 11:43 AM

< Notes

July 12, 2015

I don't know why I don't write everyday. Maybe it's because I feel so "regular" that everything is so anticlimactic.

The text to my BFF a few days ago warranted a phone call from her and her immediately telling me that I was having a panic attack. I've had anxiety attacks before and I knew exactly what was happening, but this time was different. Scary and different. So different that I couldn't recognize it. So different that it actually caused me to panic.

I had always wondered what the difference between an anxiety attack and a panic attack was. After a couple of years in psychology classes and Google, I came to the conclusion that the terms were interchangeable. But after experiencing what I

•••○○ Sprint LTE

< **Notes**

experienced, I know that is no longer the case.

Today, I woke up feeling the same tinge of anxiety. I pray this will be all there is.

I just want to be fixed.

•••oo Sprint LTE 10:47 AM

< Notes

July 14, 2015

Ok. Onion time.

When I decided to start writing, I was (and still am) very unsure of who would read my words. Like most of my interactions in life as of late, I held back a lot about myself. I'm not sure what the fear is exactly, since it's pretty much a mashup of everything.

Fear of rejection. Fear of being a bother. Fear of being seen as an imposter. Fear of not doing or saying the right things. Fear of acceptance. Fear of others' perceptions of me. Fear of not being true to myself. Fear of wasting time. Fear of not being valuable.

It's just so much.

Time to start peeling the layers.

Why do I have these fears? Are they legit?

•••○○ Sprint LTE 11:26 AM

< Notes

July 10, 2015

Where do they come from? After speaking with my psychologist, it's safe to say that these feelings come from a childhood of rejection. A childhood where I wasn't allowed to experience being a child because it put a strain on the adults in my life. Now, as an adult, I'm starting to reap what was sown.

I want to become this independent woman who has her life together, but I can't because I'm conflicting with the childhood experience of being rejected. It's a bad cycle I'm in and one of these characters has to win. The question is, which one? :-/

•••○○ Sprint LTE 11:07 AM

< Notes

July 14, 2015

I don't have my meds.

I took them with me yesterday when I went to see my therapist since I was running late. I took the pill and left the bottle in the car. Today, I let someone borrow my car and didn't realize the pills were gone until it was too late.

Now, I'm sitting on my bed kinda freaking out. My pill time is by 10:30am. I'm way past that and instead of me being calm like, *"it's okay. They will be back soon and I can just take it then. No biggie. Plus, it's only the second time you've missed a dose. It's fine."*

But, noooo...

I'm being very OCD with it. At least I *have* been. Same time. Same food. Same tea.

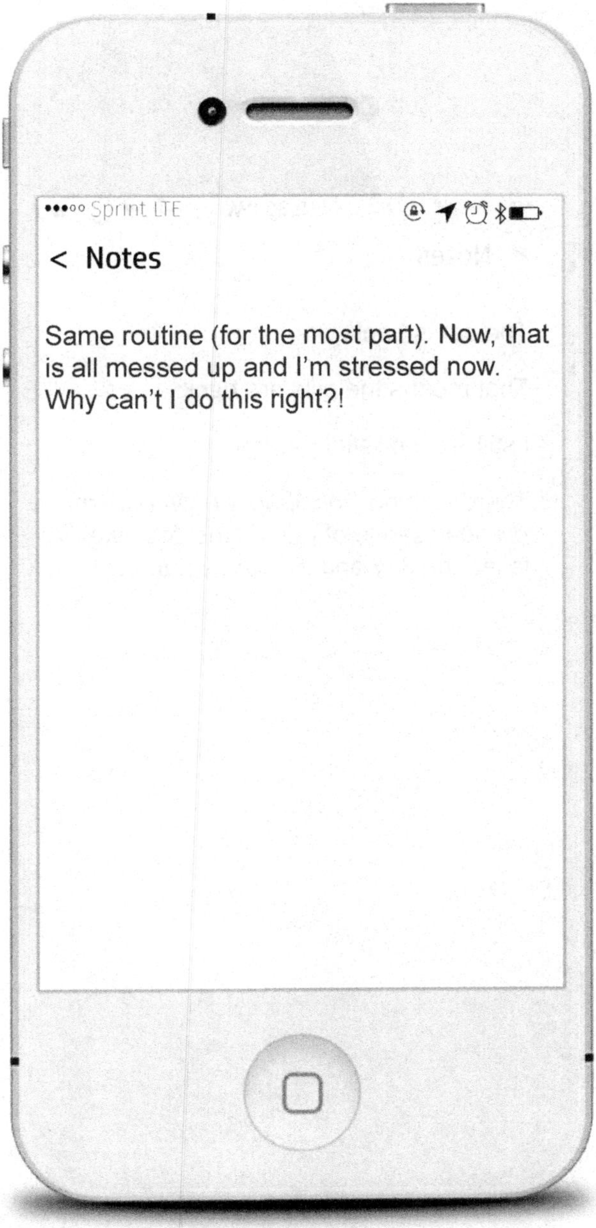
•••○○ Sprint LTE
< Notes
Same routine (for the most part). Now, that is all messed up and I'm stressed now. Why can't I do this right?!

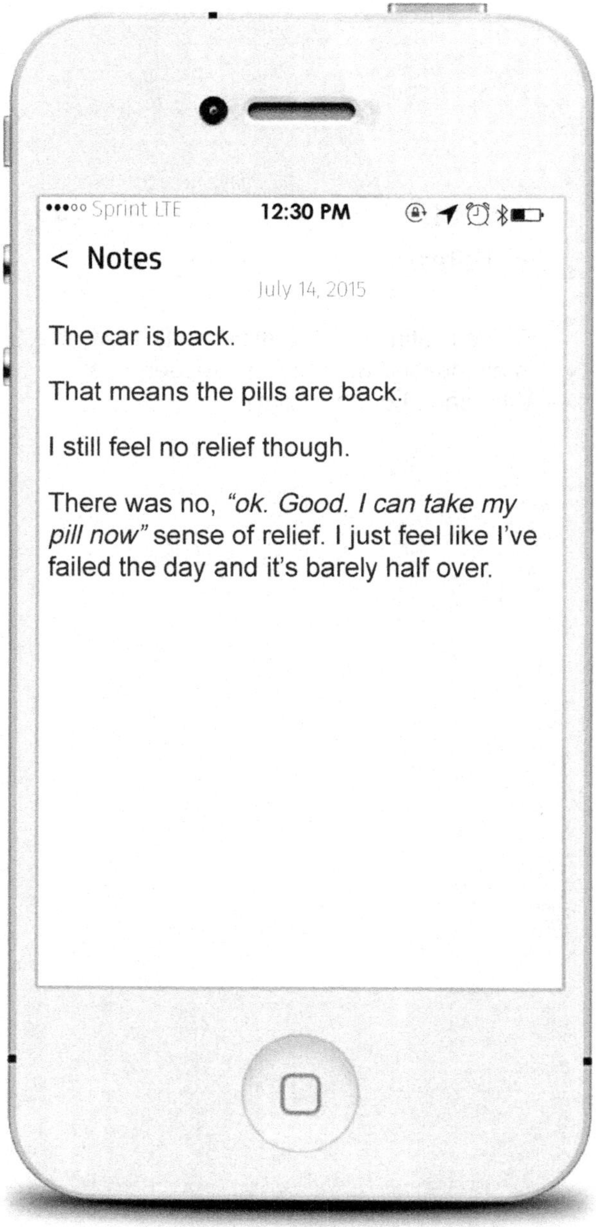
•••○○ Sprint LTE
12:30 PM
< Notes
July 14, 2015
The car is back.
That means the pills are back.
I still feel no relief though.
There was no, *"ok. Good. I can take my pill now"* sense of relief. I just feel like I've failed the day and it's barely half over.

•••○○ Sprint LTE 8:29 PM

< Notes

JULY 15, 2015

Another day and I made it out of the house. Didn't last long though.

Aat least I made the effort. Leaving the house is such a task. It feels as though things are getting worse and I have no idea where I will end up. This process is actually pretty scary. I don't understand how people go through this every day and still be okay.

Today was the day I left home thinking everything would be alright,, but, no. Aas soon as I pulled out of the driveway, I needed the day to be over.

I just want to cry hysterically.

But, I won't.

Because I don't cry.

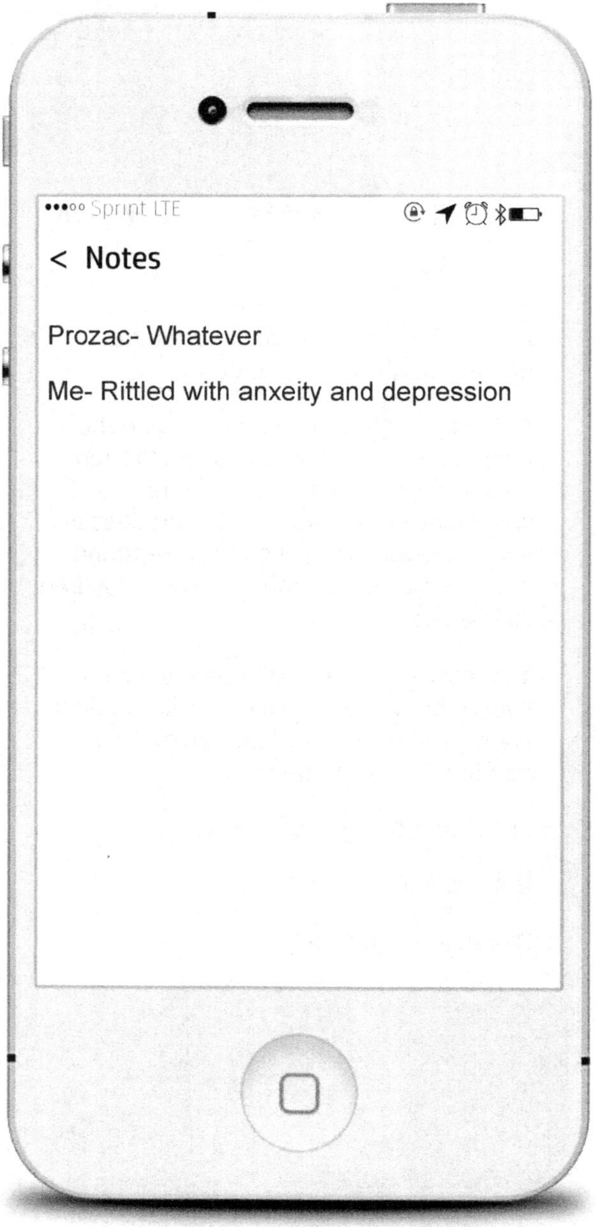
●●●○○ Sprint LTE
< Notes
Prozac- Whatever
Me- Rittled with anxiety and depression

••••○○ Sprint LTE 11:03 AM

< Notes

July 16, 2015

So far, today feels good.

Nothing special has happened except the fact that maybe the pills are finally taking affect?

This awesome!

To put it into perspective, today feels like a day where I can appreciate the sunshine and smile at everyone who comes my way. I feel like I need to be in a tampon commercial where the girl is running through a field of flowers, just frolicking.

Yes. I feel that good.

I need to frolick.

I'm ready to frolick.

•••oo Sprint LTE 1:17 PM

< Notes

July 16, 2015

I'm still laying in bed.

After yesterday's "feel good day" I am completely drained. It's like I have these "up" days and they are amazing, but then the day after, I totally crash.

I haven't taken my medicine yet, but I feel okay. Does this mean I don't need it???

I literally have not gotten out of my bed yet. Not to use the bathroom, not to drink tea, not to stretch. Nothing. I'm comfy, but I know I have to take this pill soon.

Mild OCD-like dependence on a little capsule to change your life.

:-/

●●●○○ Sprint LTE 11:43 PM

< **Notes**

July 17, 2015

I stayed up for most of the night talking with my best guy friend on FaceTime while drinking wine (I know. I know.). He knows about my mental health situation so I felt comfortable speaking to him about life lately. I've known him since I started college way back when in 2006 and he has always been my confidant. I don't know what it is, but he usually makes me feel better about everything. I wish I could carry him around in my back pocket all the time along with a flask of cheap pink moscato.

Overall, yesterday was a good day. Still not as perfect as last Tuesday, but it was good. I cleaned my room and did laundry. A+ for productivity and self-care!

As for today, meds have been taken, start-

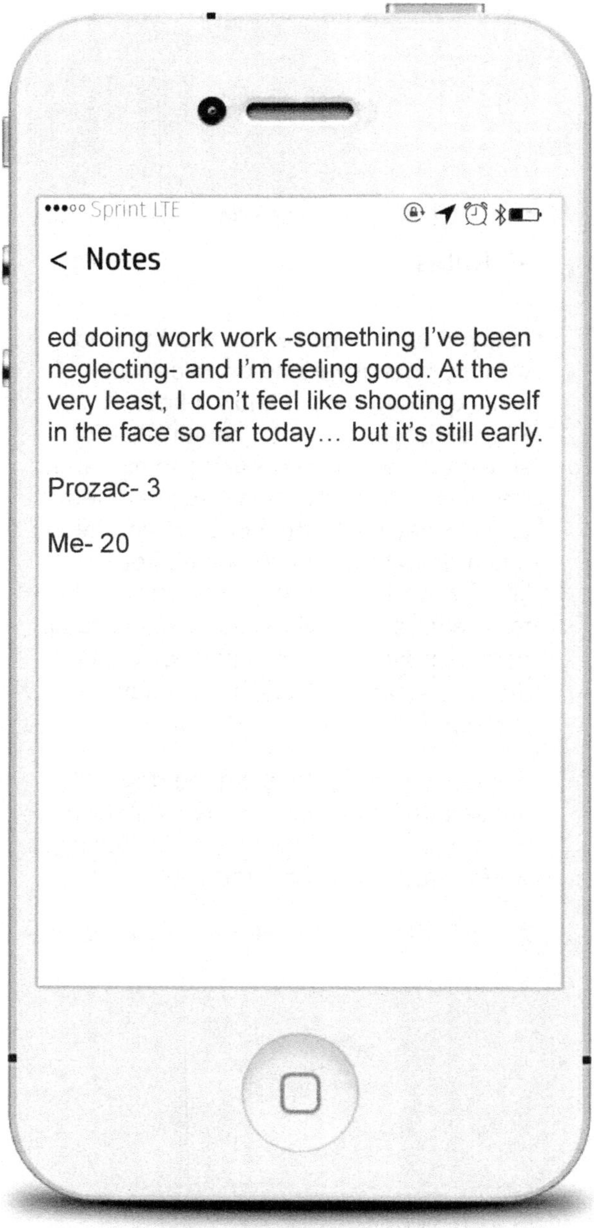

●●●○○ Sprint LTE
< Notes
ed doing work work -something I've been neglecting- and I'm feeling good. At the very least, I don't feel like shooting myself in the face so far today… but it's still early.
Prozac- 3
Me- 20

•••○○ Sprint LTE 10: 47 PM

< Notes

July 18, 2015

Today was a good day! Surprisingly. After waking up contemplating my life, I had to go out and be personable. At first it was very hard. I was on the brink of a panic attack while in the midst of a few hundred people in one place. But I was able to move through it. Later, I ended up at an adult water ballon fight. Great laughs.

I did good today.

Let's see how long this streak will last.

••••○○ Sprint LTE 11:03 PM

< **Notes**

July 19, 2015

I'm so tired.

Physically and mentally. I feel drained. I'm ready for real change to come.

Late on the pill- again. Oh well. I don't even care anymore.

Again, It feels like when I have a good day, it's followed by a miserable day. I day where things aren't looking up. A day where I question everything. Is this even worth it? I'm going through the trouble of therapy and taking medicine for only one good day?

I really am not seeing the benefit. But I guess one day is better than no days. So, that's a plus, I guess.

●●●○○ Sprint LTE
7:54 PM
< Notes
July 19, 2015
I legit slept all day. I feel like crap. Just thinking about life as usual.

•••○○ Sprint LTE 9:26 PM

< Notes

July 20, 2015

I saw my psychologist today. The session went well and I wish it could have lasted longer. To make a long story short, we came to a conclusion that I have an issue with losing control or being out of control.

CONTROL?!

I've never had a problem with dealing with control- at least not to a recognizable point- I've always been very put together and everything must be "just so." Not quite the control freak, right? But I'm glad to have something come to light and now I can work on it.

Now, as for my destructive obsessive thoughts… definitely something to keep an eye on as I continue to take medication.

I still feel debilitating anxiety and have

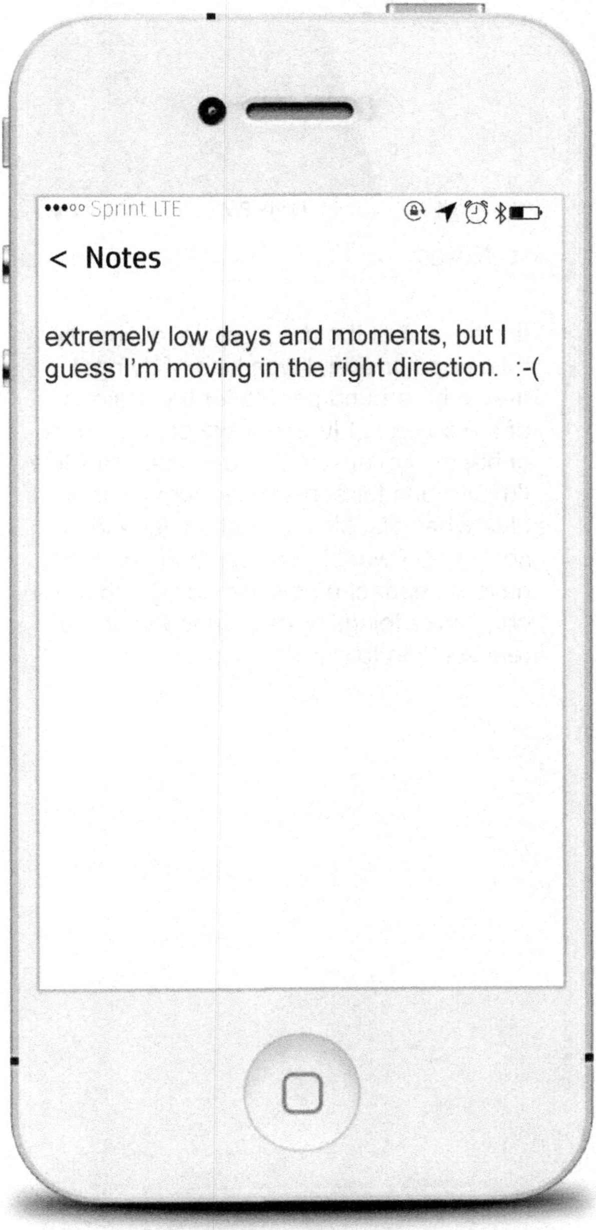
•••○○ Sprint LTE
< Notes
extremely low days and moments, but I guess I'm moving in the right direction. :-(

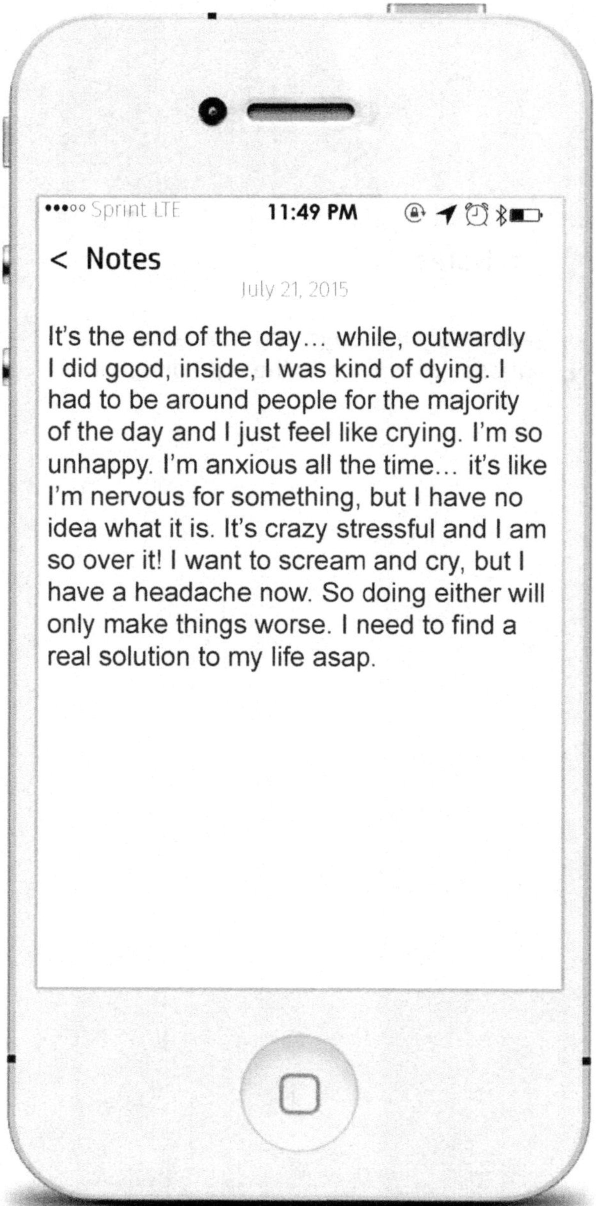

•••oo Sprint LTE
11:49 PM
< Notes
July 21, 2015
It's the end of the day… while, outwardly I did good, inside, I was kind of dying. I had to be around people for the majority of the day and I just feel like crying. I'm so unhappy. I'm anxious all the time… it's like I'm nervous for something, but I have no idea what it is. It's crazy stressful and I am so over it! I want to scream and cry, but I have a headache now. So doing either will only make things worse. I need to find a real solution to my life asap.

●●●○○ Sprint LTE 10:15 AM

< Notes

July 22, 2015

Is it bad that I want my own space? My own place? I am currently living with other people, and to be frank, my life is pretty free and clear. I don't have to pay for any bills, so I know I should be grateful and appreciative, but I'm not. I just want to be by myself in my own apartment. Problem is, I can't. Because I have no income. I have no money. So I'm stuck. I'm just so tired of having to make sure the others are comfortable and that I'm not in their space. It's so tiresome. It's also so sad that at this age I can't support myself. I need to figure this thing out quick. I don't want to live like this on other people's terms.

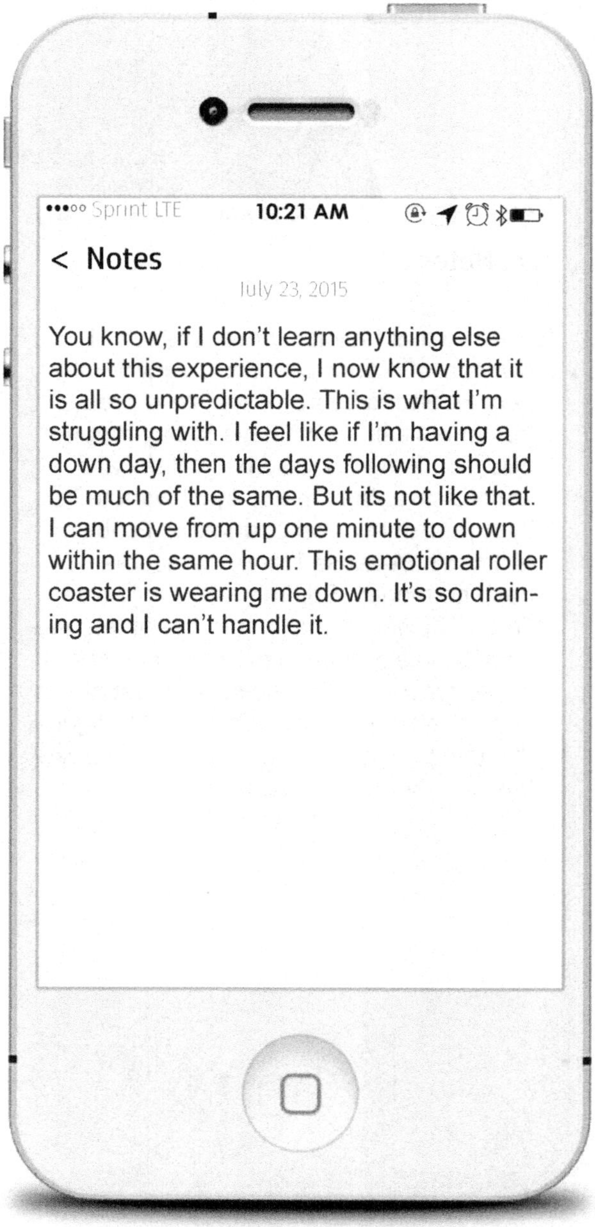
•••oo Sprint LTE
10:21 AM
< Notes
July 23, 2015
You know, if I don't learn anything else about this experience, I now know that it is all so unpredictable. This is what I'm struggling with. I feel like if I'm having a down day, then the days following should be much of the same. But its not like that. I can move from up one minute to down within the same hour. This emotional roller coaster is wearing me down. It's so draining and I can't handle it.

●●●○○ Sprint LTE
10:03 AM
< Notes
July 24, 2015
I actually took a shower today. :'-(

•••oo Sprint LTE 11:06 AM

< Notes

July 24, 2015

Today I took my last pill of my first bottle. 30th pill.

Sigh.

I managed to take the pills everyday for a month without missing any days. I honestly can't believe I stuck it out and was so diligent about it. I just *knew* that after day 5, I was done. But, I guess when you have come to your last resort, you do what you can to see it through.

Looking back on this month, I had some really amazing days and I had some very, very dark days. Yes, my down days overwhelmed my up days, by far, but the fact that I even had full good days is a win. :-/

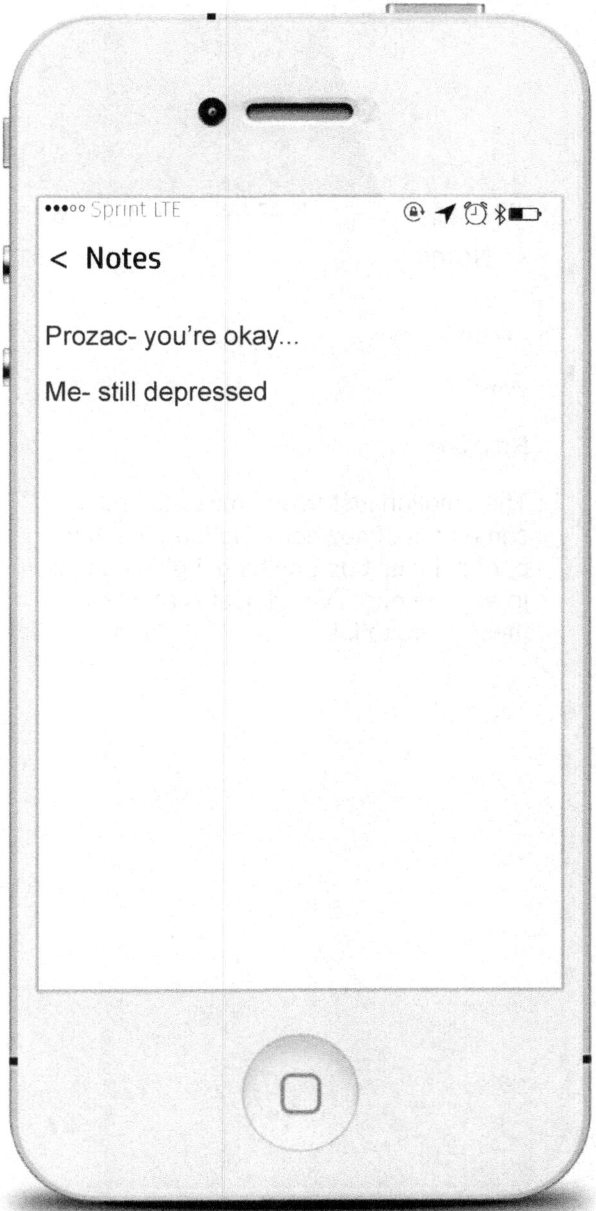

Sprint LTE
< Notes
Prozac- you're okay...
Me- still depressed

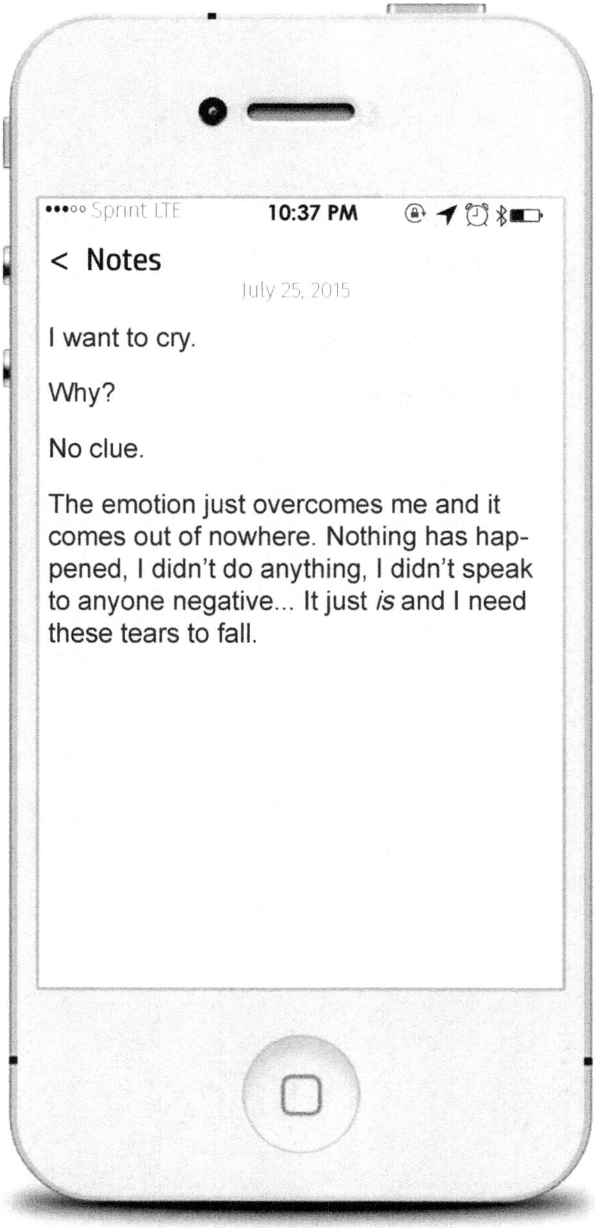
•••○○ Sprint LTE
10:37 PM
< Notes
July 25, 2015
I want to cry.
Why?
No clue.
The emotion just overcomes me and it comes out of nowhere. Nothing has happened, I didn't do anything, I didn't speak to anyone negative... It just *is* and I need these tears to fall.

•••oo Sprint LTE 6:30 PM

< Notes

July 26, 2015

I tried. I really did. I did the people thing. I interacted. I spoke. I even hugged people. Now, I'm just tired. During all of that, I was definitely having an anxiety attack, so I left. I went and stood outside and waited for my ride to be ready to leave.

I want to cry so bad right now.

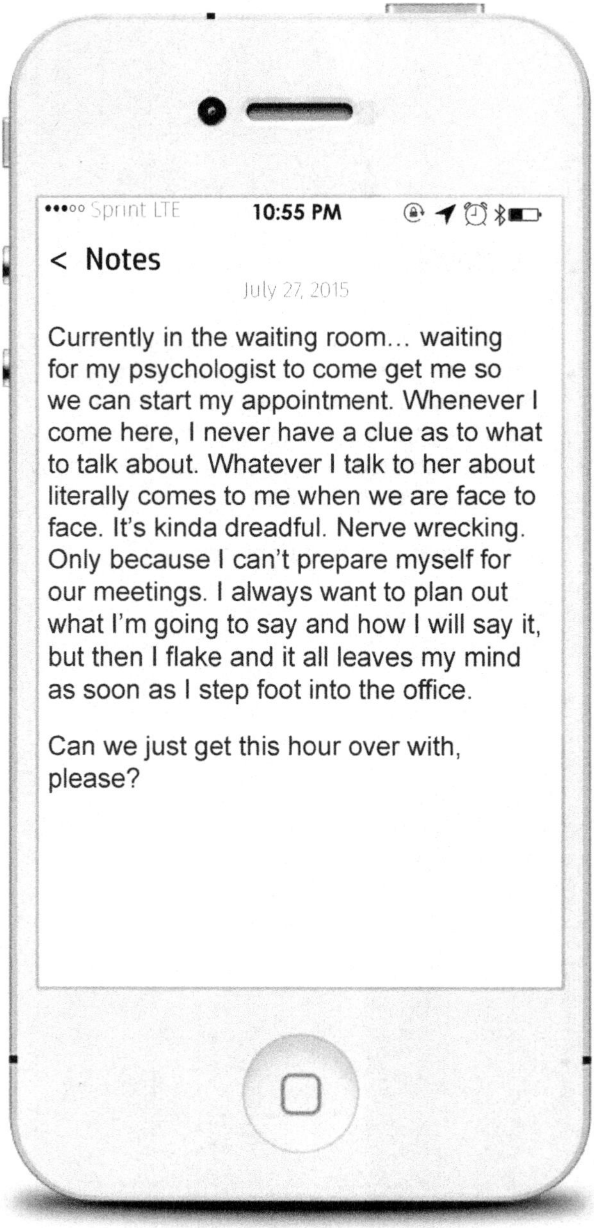
•••○○ Sprint LTE 10:55 PM

< Notes

July 27, 2015

Currently in the waiting room… waiting for my psychologist to come get me so we can start my appointment. Whenever I come here, I never have a clue as to what to talk about. Whatever I talk to her about literally comes to me when we are face to face. It's kinda dreadful. Nerve wrecking. Only because I can't prepare myself for our meetings. I always want to plan out what I'm going to say and how I will say it, but then I flake and it all leaves my mind as soon as I step foot into the office.

Can we just get this hour over with, please?

•••oo Sprint LTE 1:07 PM

< Notes

July 28, 2015

Everytime I come from seeing the doctor I am completely drained. It takes so much out of me to open up and just *talk*. You would think I had just ran a marathon.

My psychiatrist canceled our follow up appointment that was scheduled for tomorrow. It kind of distressed me because I had *planned* to go.

Like, *tthis isn't the plan!!* I quickly got over it, but the fact that it freaked me out that the plan changed… that's not good.

I theoretically understand OCD, but now I feel like I'm breaking through the surface of it myself.

Another thing to add to the checklist of things to talk about… The checklist I never use.

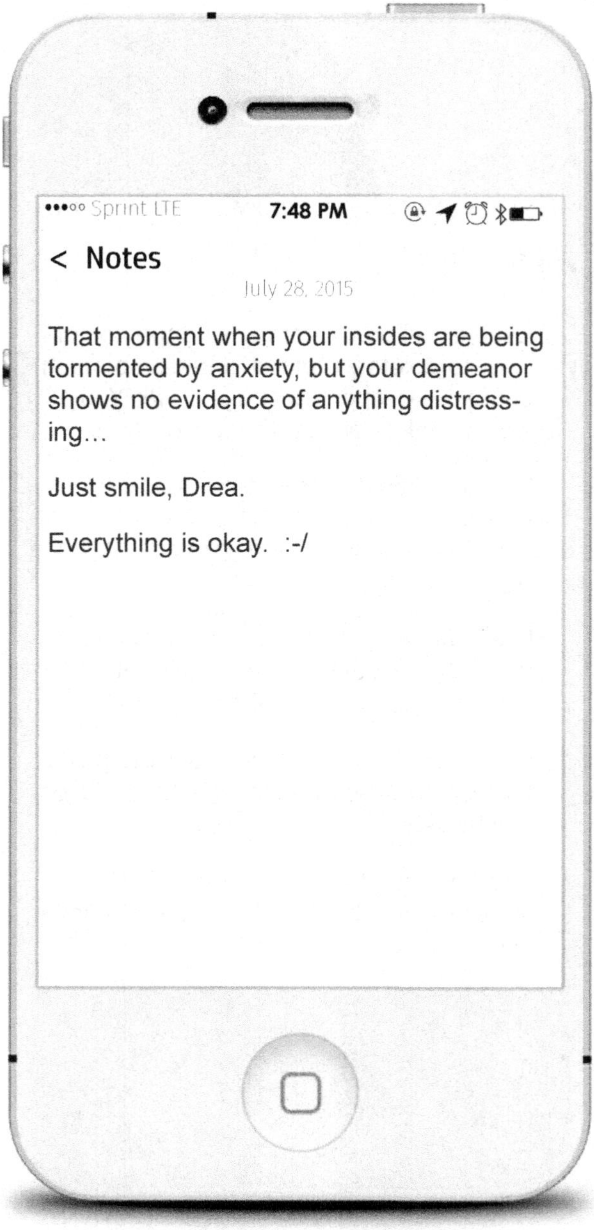
•••○○ Sprint LTE
7:48 PM
< Notes
July 28, 2015
That moment when your insides are being tormented by anxiety, but your demeanor shows no evidence of anything distressing…
Just smile, Drea.
Everything is okay. :-/

•••○○ Sprint LTE 10:51 PM

< **Notes**

July 30, 2015

I haven't taken my medicine yet. I'm actually out of the house right now and don't have immediate access to food, so Zach (my nickname for Prozac) will have to wait a bit. I'm not feeling good today at all though. So far, I want to slit my wrists.

Sigh.

Looking forward to having another actual "good" day. When does *that* come back?

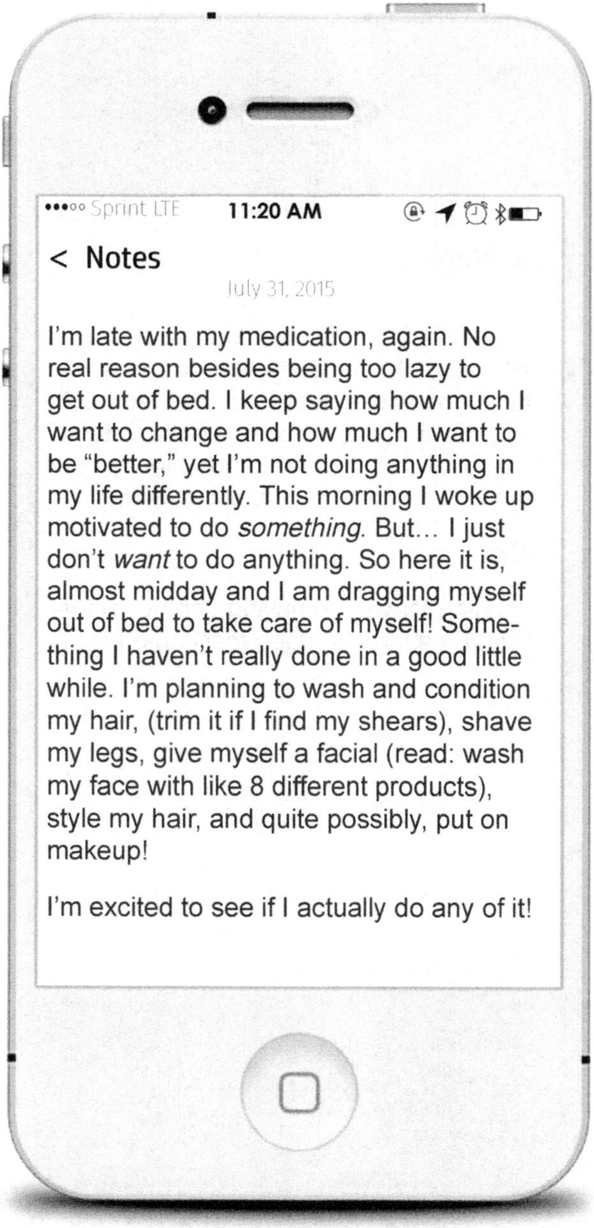

•••oo Sprint LTE
11:20 AM
< Notes
July 31, 2015
I'm late with my medication, again. No real reason besides being too lazy to get out of bed. I keep saying how much I want to change and how much I want to be "better," yet I'm not doing anything in my life differently. This morning I woke up motivated to do *something*. But… I just don't *want* to do anything. So here it is, almost midday and I am dragging myself out of bed to take care of myself! Something I haven't really done in a good little while. I'm planning to wash and condition my hair, (trim it if I find my shears), shave my legs, give myself a facial (read: wash my face with like 8 different products), style my hair, and quite possibly, put on makeup!
I'm excited to see if I actually do any of it!

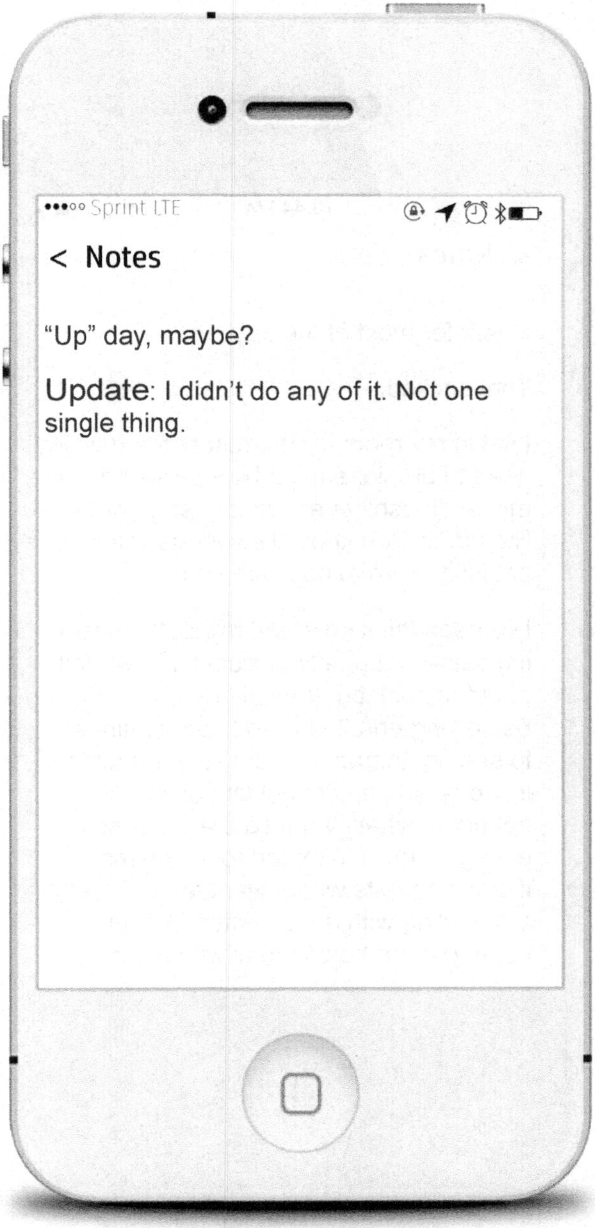
●●●○○ Sprint LTE
< Notes
"Up" day, maybe?
Update: I didn't do any of it. Not one single thing.

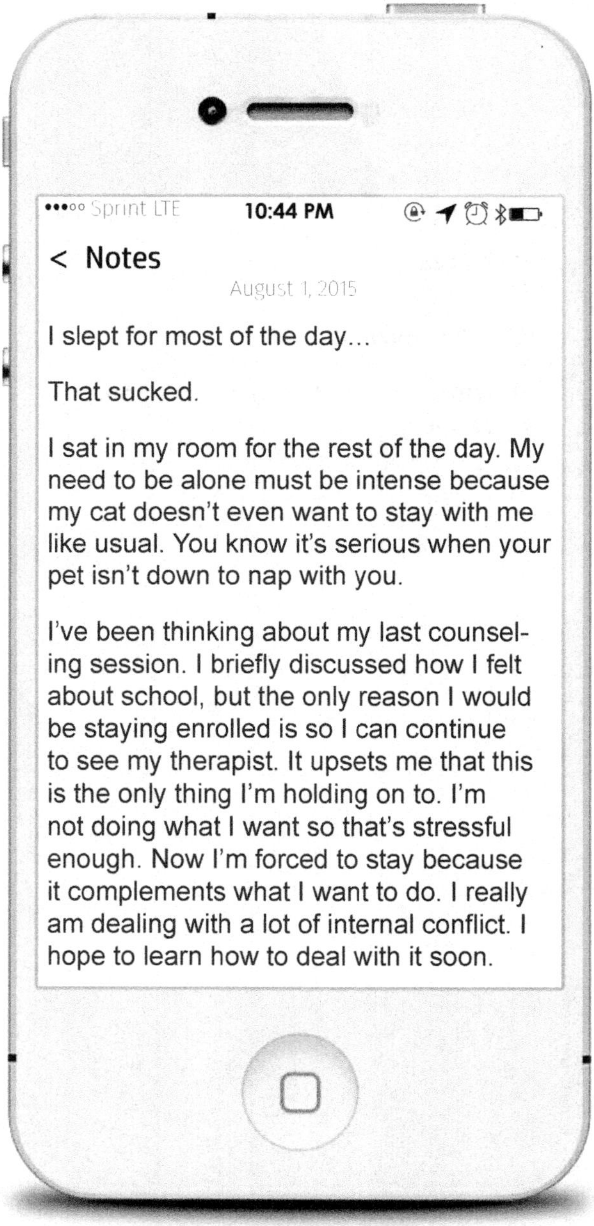

I slept for most of the day...

That sucked.

I sat in my room for the rest of the day. My need to be alone must be intense because my cat doesn't even want to stay with me like usual. You know it's serious when your pet isn't down to nap with you.

I've been thinking about my last counseling session. I briefly discussed how I felt about school, but the only reason I would be staying enrolled is so I can continue to see my therapist. It upsets me that this is the only thing I'm holding on to. I'm not doing what I want so that's stressful enough. Now I'm forced to stay because it complements what I want to do. I really am dealing with a lot of internal conflict. I hope to learn how to deal with it soon.

●●●○○ Sprint LTE
< Notes
It's all just a means to an end, Drea. Just deal with it.

August 3, 2015

Monday.

I'm currently laying in the bed reading the beginning-of- the-week-motivational-instagram-quotes asking why they aren't motivating me to be productive.

Sigh.

But, for what it's worth, I'm excited to go see my psychologist today. I don't know what *that's* about.

Why am I... *excited*????????????

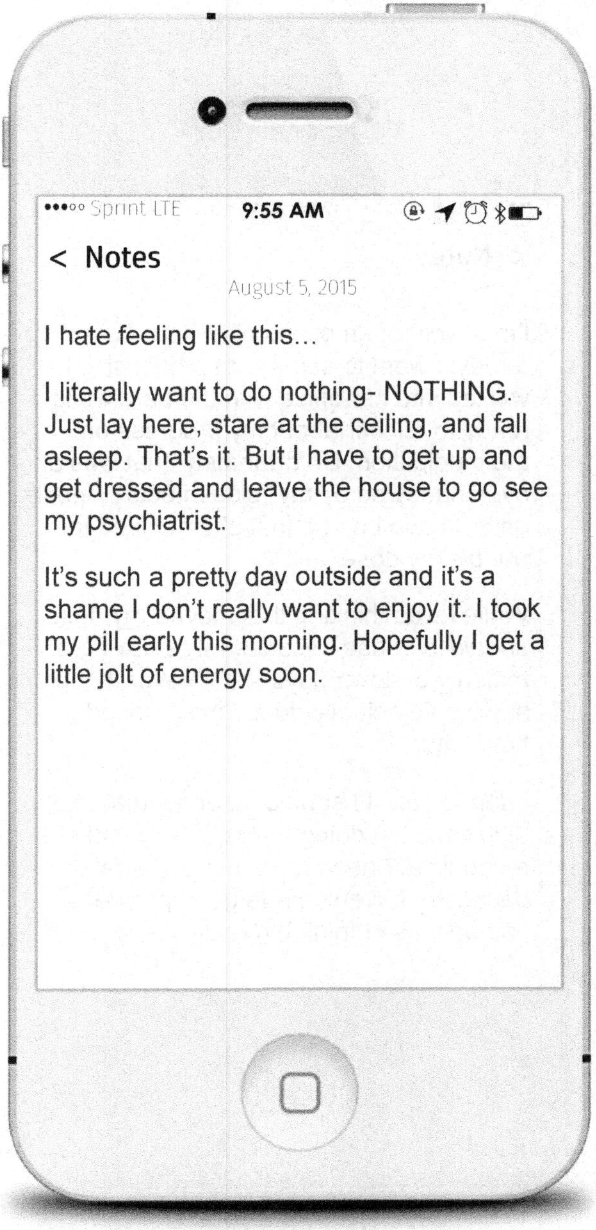
•••oo Sprint LTE
9:55 AM
< Notes
August 5, 2015
I hate feeling like this…
I literally want to do nothing- NOTHING. Just lay here, stare at the ceiling, and fall asleep. That's it. But I have to get up and get dressed and leave the house to go see my psychiatrist.
It's such a pretty day outside and it's a shame I don't really want to enjoy it. I took my pill early this morning. Hopefully I get a little jolt of energy soon.

•••○○ Sprint LTE 9:00 AM

< **Notes**

August 6, 2015

I'm a whirl of emotions right now. Yesterday, I went to see the psychiatrist… I walked into her office with the bare walls ready to tell her about my progress on the medication. Unfortunately, that was all overshadowed by my "side effects". Apparently, I'm so bad off that she decided to *double* my dose.

While I was thinking that maybe my dose *should* increase because I was having a majority of down days still, I never thought she would actually do it. I'm surprised, honestly.

I don't know if I should be upset that she didn't see I'm doing better, happy that she recognized I need more help, frustrated because I haven't made good progress, sad because I think I'm really crazy… It's

•••oo Sprint LTE

< Notes

just too much right now.

I haven't showered in a few days and Mother Nature has officially returned. So I guess it's time. I'll take a moment to wash away my feelings and accept that *this* is now a part of my life and is here to stay.

At least for now.

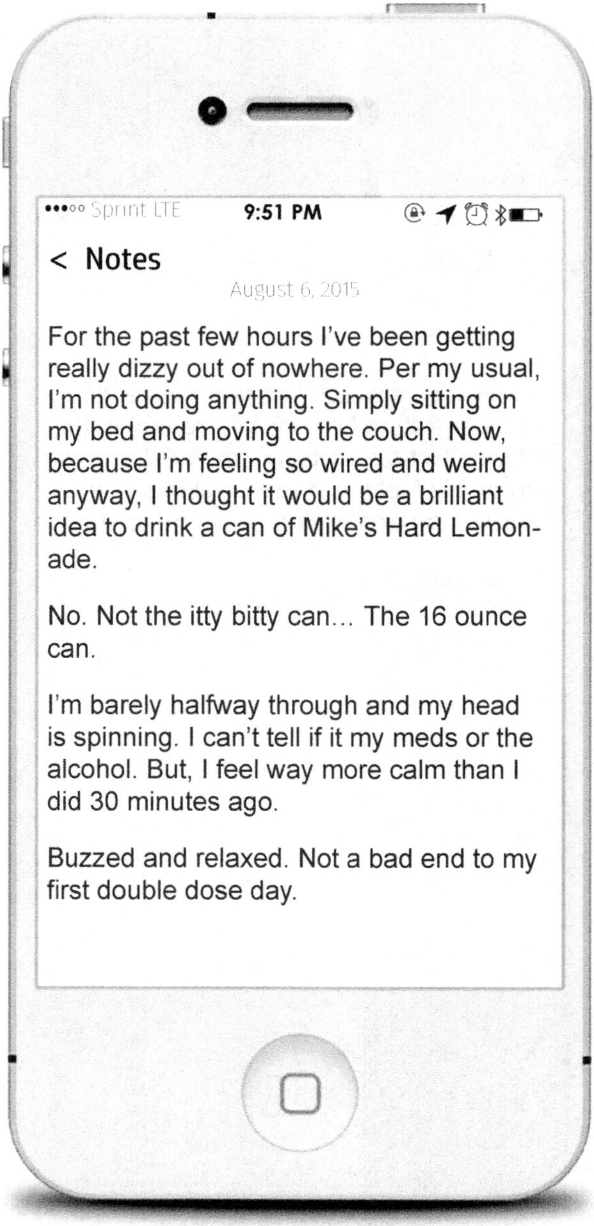
Sprint LTE
9:51 PM
< Notes
August 6, 2015
For the past few hours I've been getting really dizzy out of nowhere. Per my usual, I'm not doing anything. Simply sitting on my bed and moving to the couch. Now, because I'm feeling so wired and weird anyway, I thought it would be a brilliant idea to drink a can of Mike's Hard Lemonade.
No. Not the itty bitty can… The 16 ounce can.
I'm barely halfway through and my head is spinning. I can't tell if it my meds or the alcohol. But, I feel way more calm than I did 30 minutes ago.
Buzzed and relaxed. Not a bad end to my first double dose day.

•••○○ Sprint LTE 12:47 PM

< **Notes**

August 13, 2015

It's been a while. I think I may be coming closer to the end of the road for me... After being on this higher dose of medication for about a week now, I can honestly say I feel like a totally different person... in a good way.

...Barring all side effects, of course.

None the less, I feel quite amazing to have come from such a dark place a few months ago. Because of this positive drastic change, my psychologist sees it fit for us to move a bi-weekly session. In truth, I was very nervous when she told me. I was like, "Nope. I'm good. Why mess up a good thing?!" But now that I have thought about it, it would make sense.

I have 7 sessions left.

•••○○ Sprint LTE

< Notes

If I continue to go weekly, that puts me at the end of September. If I move to biweekly, essentially, I get 14 more weeks of treatment, which will bring me all the way to the end of the semester.

If I stick to weekly and something happens mid-semester and I need to see her, I'm screwed.

If I go bi-weekly an something happens, I'll have the option available to meet with her if I need to.

Because I'm a worrywart and I need to feel safe and secure in the decision I make, next week I will tell her that I want to go to a biweekly schedule. I'm confident that I'm doing so well, I think I can manage the change. It only works if you work it!

Sprint LTE
< Notes
Here's to a great semester!

•••○○ Sprint LTE 11:12 AM

< Notes

August 15, 2015

Do medical/clinical doctors go through some type of psychological class that teaches them to not self-diagnose?!

Going through my psychiatric/ psychological treatment and having *some* prior knowledge of the DSM (Diagnostic and Statistical Manual of Mental Disorders) and having a natural tendency to research everything, I feel the need to diagnose myself with other disorders.

Cue: *body dysmorphic disorder.*

Since I could remember, I have always had a tough time with my appearance. I hated my boobs, my butt could stand to be a little rounder, my abs needed to be toned in a very soft, feminine way, my hair just sucked and I need a weave to feel good, my eyebrows don't have a natural

•••○○ Sprint LTE

< Notes

arch but I can't draw them on because they are dumb thick, my hands and feet are too skinny, my thighs are too big, I have a ridiculous amount of back fat to be "small", I have smile lines and neck rolls, my top lip is longer than my bottom lip giving me a permanent frown, let's not even get into my teeth, my skin blows with the adult acne and all of the dark spots and scabs that I continuously pick at, my eyes are dark and sunken in, and sometimes I feel like I smell.

Yeah, everyone has flaws, *blah blah blah*... But does everyone pick at their "flaws" every time they see them or think about them or when they see others *without* said flaws?! Like, I look up breast augmentations EVERY DAY, studying size and shape before and after surgery, comparing the patient's stats to mine. I do everything in my power to take care of my skin, but thinking about it makes me scratch and pick even more. It's just a bad cycle. If that isn't *BDD*, I don't know what is.

But that's the thing...

I *DON'T* know what it is.

I'm not a doctor-- PhD, MD, nor DO. I have no clue of the scientific basis of diagnosing this disorder. But me being me, yearning to eventually become a doctor, I read between the lines of symptoms and treatments and causes, trying to make my own meaning based off articles on Web-MD and results form Google. It doesn't make sense as to why I do this.

I hope that once I *do* become a doctor

•••○○ Sprint LTE

< Notes

(MD or otherwise), I don't feel the need to self-diagnose. It is so draining.

Here's to my BDD…

My personality may now be A1, but my body and self image is trash.

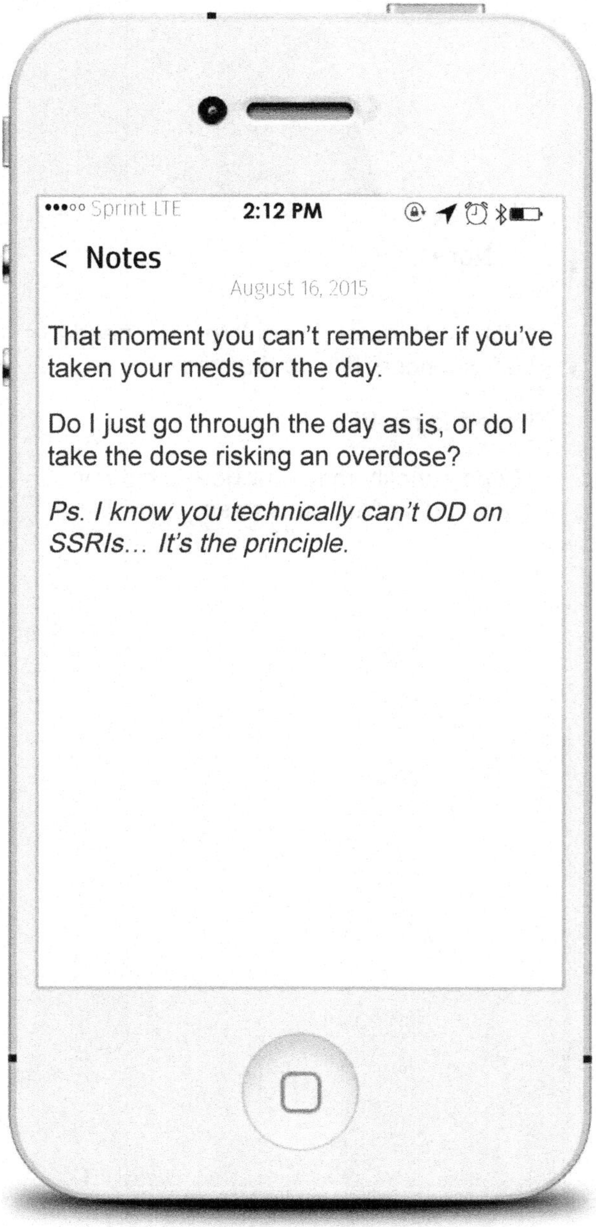

•••○○ Sprint LTE
2:12 PM
< Notes
August 16, 2015
That moment you can't remember if you've taken your meds for the day.
Do I just go through the day as is, or do I take the dose risking an overdose?
Ps. I know you technically can't OD on SSRIs… It's the principle.

•••○○ Sprint LTE 11:45 AM

< Notes

August 21, 2015

Sigh.

After making such amazing progress, I still feel stuck. I'm "up" a lot more, but the anxiety sucks.

●●●○○ Sprint LTE 9:02 PM

< Notes

August 28, 2015

I don't know when the shift happened, but it happened… In a quiet gradual yet abrupt way. It's barely been 2 months and I actually feel amazing! Somewhere inbetween my last update and now I have been to Costa Rica, zip lined across a rainforest, hiked to several waterfalls on the side of a mountain, rode a horse through a herd of bulls, and interacted with strangers in close quarters.

The fact that I said yes to something as intense as this trip is still unbelievable!

Like, I went to a foreign country "by myself" (I had a best friend waiting for me when I got off the plane), talked to people I didn't know, and even made an attempt to converse in Spanish. I really can't believe it…

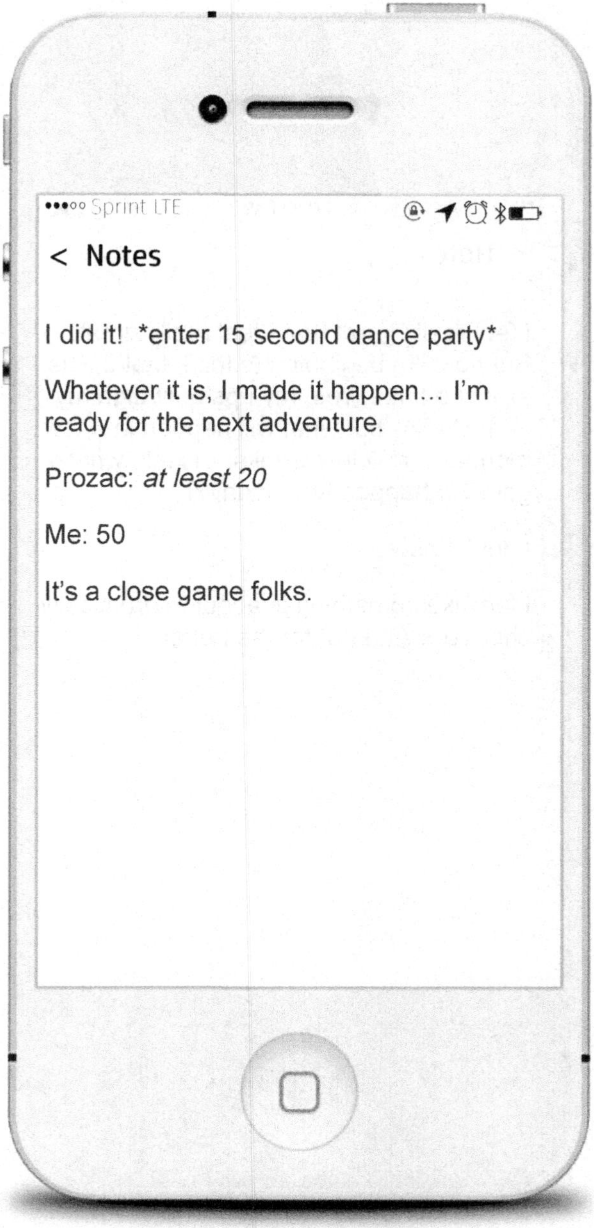
●●●○○ Sprint LTE
< Notes
I did it! *enter 15 second dance party*
Whatever it is, I made it happen… I'm ready for the next adventure.
Prozac: *at least 20*
Me: 50
It's a close game folks.

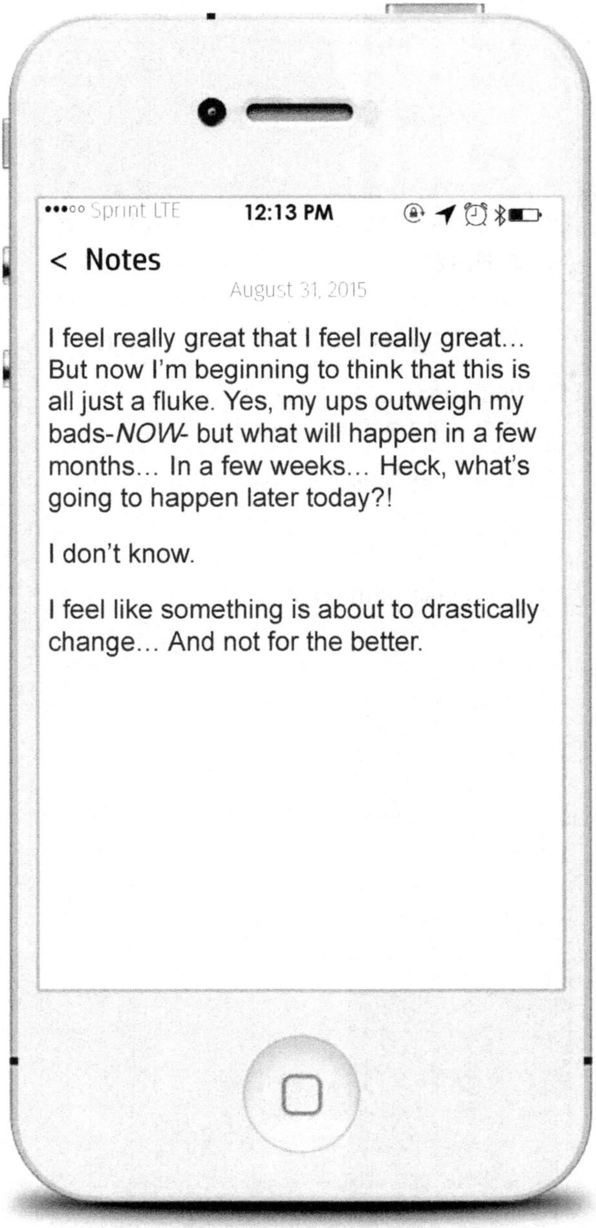
Sprint LTE
12:13 PM
< Notes
August 31, 2015
I feel really great that I feel really great... But now I'm beginning to think that this is all just a fluke. Yes, my ups outweigh my bads-*NOW*- but what will happen in a few months... In a few weeks... Heck, what's going to happen later today?!
I don't know.
I feel like something is about to drastically change... And not for the better.

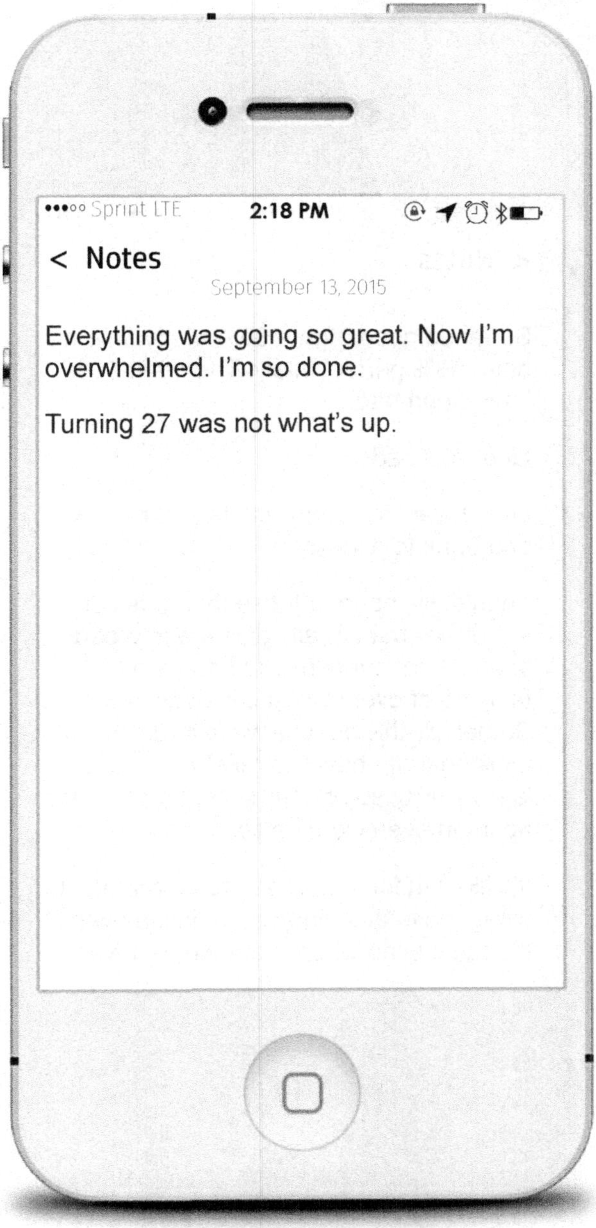
Sprint LTE
2:18 PM
< Notes
September 13, 2015
Everything was going so great. Now I'm overwhelmed. I'm so done.
Turning 27 was not what's up.

•••○○ Sprint LTE 12:56 PM

< Notes

September 21, 2015

So far so good, right? 80% of my time has been 98% perfect lately. The other 20% have been bad.

Like, *bad* bad.

Like, I want to slit my wrists and run away and drink to excess.

Thankfully, none of those thoughts come to fruition, but it really puts me in a bad space. I get overwhelmed and start thinking of every worst case scenario. Somehow this spiral always ends with me thinking that I have no relief and that this is my reality so I better accept it or I'll end up in an even worse place.

It's like I'm forcing myself to be grateful for what I have and where I am in life even though it is no where near where I want to

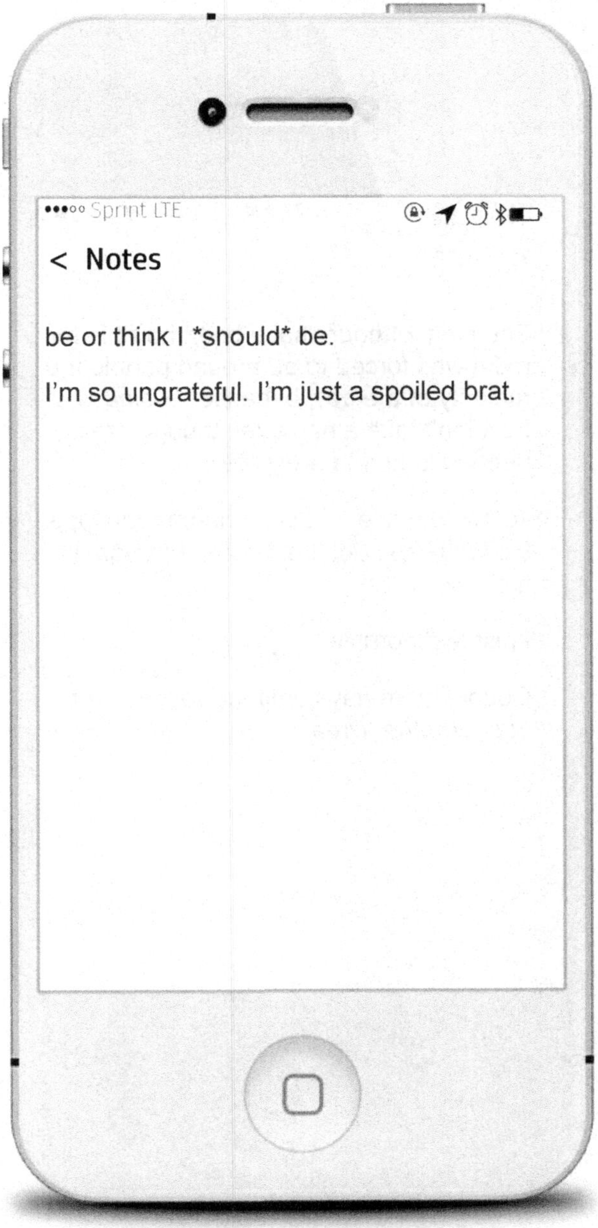
Sprint LTE
< Notes
be or think I *should* be.
I'm so ungrateful. I'm just a spoiled brat.

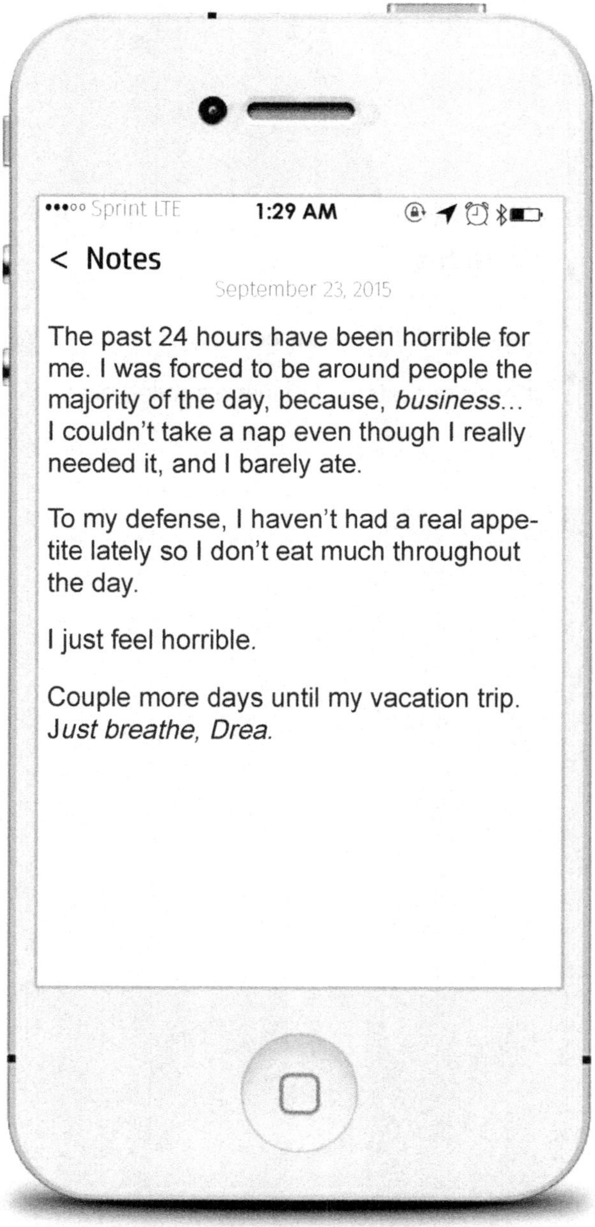

The past 24 hours have been horrible for me. I was forced to be around people the majority of the day, because, *business*... I couldn't take a nap even though I really needed it, and I barely ate.

To my defense, I haven't had a real appetite lately so I don't eat much throughout the day.

I just feel horrible.

Couple more days until my vacation trip. *Just breathe, Drea.*

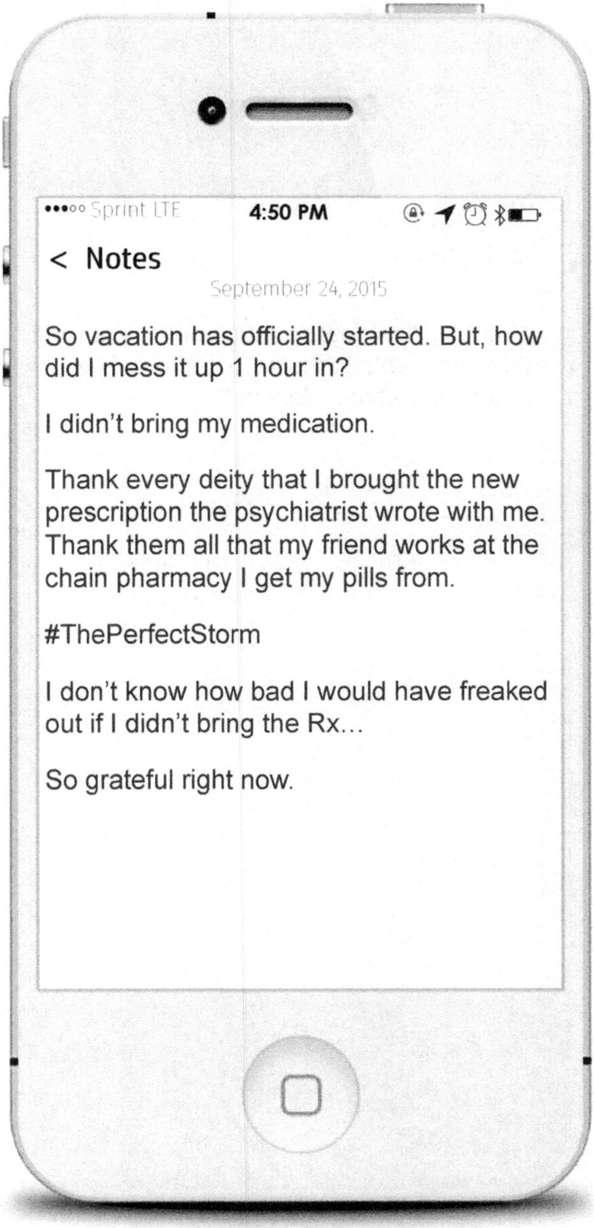
●●●○○ Sprint LTE
4:50 PM
< Notes
September 24, 2015
So vacation has officially started. But, how did I mess it up 1 hour in?
I didn't bring my medication.
Thank every deity that I brought the new prescription the psychiatrist wrote with me. Thank them all that my friend works at the chain pharmacy I get my pills from.
#ThePerfectStorm
I don't know how bad I would have freaked out if I didn't bring the Rx…
So grateful right now.

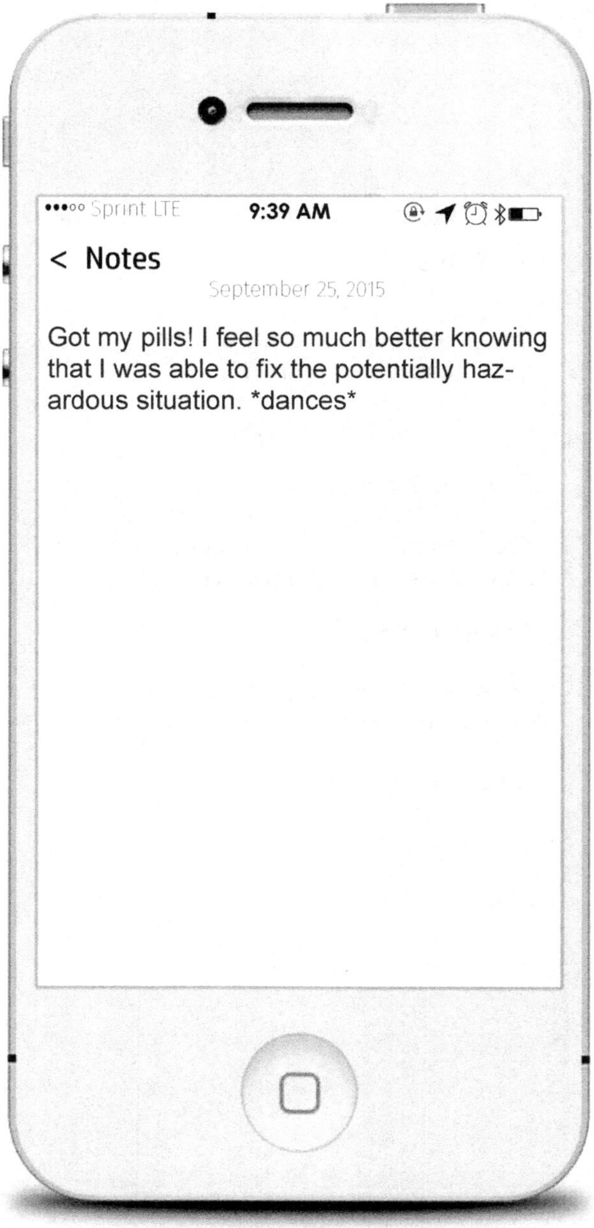
•••oo Sprint LTE
9:39 AM
< Notes
September 25, 2015
Got my pills! I feel so much better knowing that I was able to fix the potentially hazardous situation. *dances*

•••oo Sprint LTE 11:01 PM

< Notes

September 28, 2015

Vacation is going okay so far. I went to see my family, but their lack of enthusiasm when it came to seeing me after 5years was disheartening. Why do I still feel the need to be accepted? Or even that I am inadequate? I went to see my best friend's family and they were more excited to see me.

Context: I saw them a few months ago. Still a lot of positive energy.

I'm dwelling on it. Idk why.

I'm trying. I really am. I hope the trip wasn't a waste.

•••oo Sprint LTE 6:51 PM

< Notes

October 1, 2015

Still on vakay. Currently, laying in my hotel bed in the Dominican Republic. In the next bed half asleep and talking to me, is my best friend who is officially a working physician.

Any *sane* person would bask in this time away with one of their most favorite people in the world.. But me? I'm freaking out about life, as per usual.

We leave and head back to the States tomorrow so I'm wondering about what I'm going to do once I get back to Atlanta when all of this is said and done. How will I shape my life into something I love? What are my next steps when it comes to a career? School? Let's not even think about that...

I know I need to just buckle down, make a

●●●○○ Sprint LTE

< Notes

decision, and do it, but my mind is racing and at this point, so is my heart. I just want to cry right now.

I want to ugly-Kim-Kardashian-cry. That's how bad I feel.

Upside? I *don't* want to sleep.

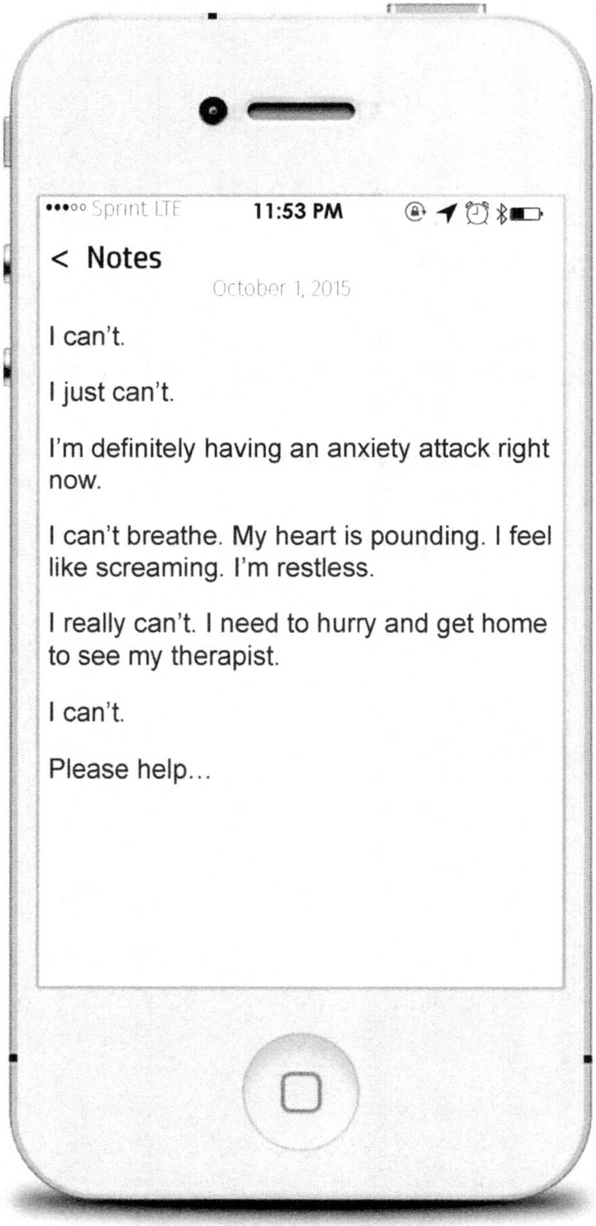
●●●○○ Sprint LTE
11:53 PM
< Notes
October 1, 2015
I can't.
I just can't.
I'm definitely having an anxiety attack right now.
I can't breathe. My heart is pounding. I feel like screaming. I'm restless.
I really can't. I need to hurry and get home to see my therapist.
I can't.
Please help…

•••○○ Sprint LTE 1:16 PM

< **Notes**

October 10, 2015

I'm trying really hard to play nice with everyone, but I feel drained and I have no idea why.

That's a lie...

I know exactly why.

I'm so irritated with my life right now. So annoyed that I'm not doing much with it. Aggravated that I can't be happy for more than 3 days at a time. It's like I'm forcing myself to lead a double life and it is taking its toll.

I just want to sleep.

•••oo Sprint LTE 11:53 PM

< Notes

October 12, 2015

Despite my physical surroundings I feel so neglected. Literally I'm the red headed step child of life. Lately I've been feeling bad and I can't put my finger on it. Yes I'm back to wanting to slit my wrists, run away, crash my car… The usual angsty teenage stuff…

But I'm not a teenager.

I'm closer to 30 than I am to 19.

Sometimes I think life is just BS when you aren't doing what you want.

I just want to drink and lay on the beach.

But noooo….

I need money. I need a job. I should be thinking of my future. I should be taking

•••oo Sprint LTE

< **Notes**

my pills. I should be playing nice with everyone.

Should should should.

It's futile.

I need something to make me feel like life is what I want… Something to feed my wanderlust and wayward spirit. I'll even take something that will ground me- as long as I enjoy it.

I just feel empty. As of right now I have no purpose. Like what am I even doing? Do I know what I want to do?

My emotions are everywhere.

I want to finally cry. I admit that I don't know anything and that I am a failure. But

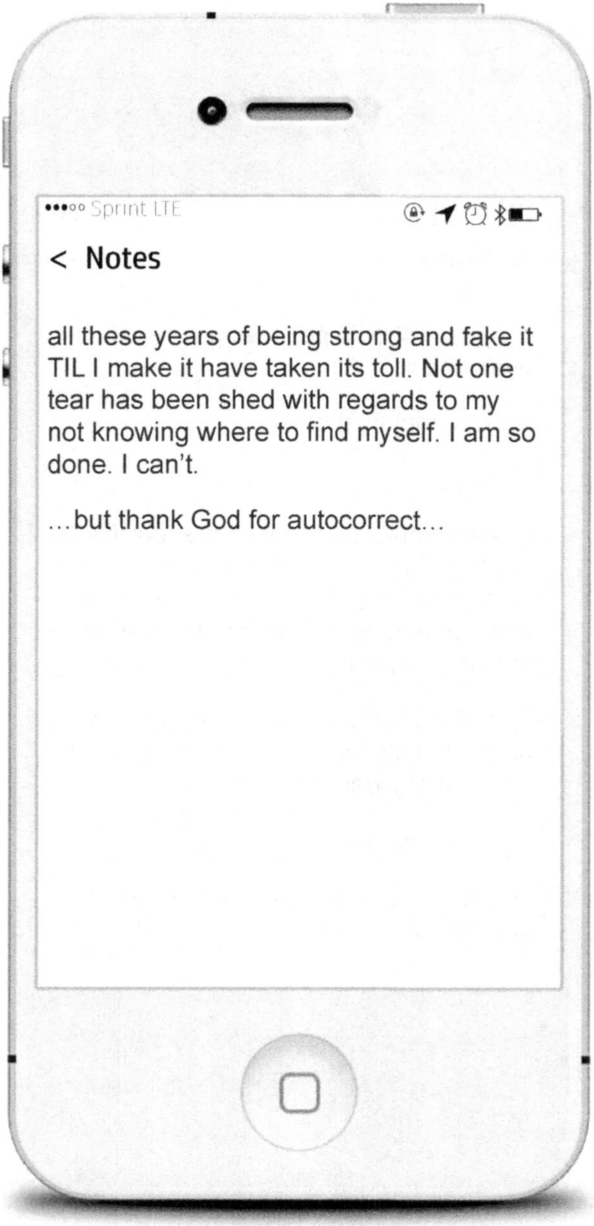
Sprint LTE
< Notes
all these years of being strong and fake it TIL I make it have taken its toll. Not one tear has been shed with regards to my not knowing where to find myself. I am so done. I can't.
...but thank God for autocorrect...

••••○○ Sprint LTE 9:52 PM

< **Notes**

October 14, 2015

I faked it today. Got work done and interacted. I'm beat. I need wine. My heart still feels like it's about to come out my chest. I haven't had caffeine so that's not it.

Wtf is wrong with me?

I feel like I need to *feel* something. Like the movie "Crash". I need a jolt of something to wake me up. To make me alive. To make me happy. I hate floating and zoning.

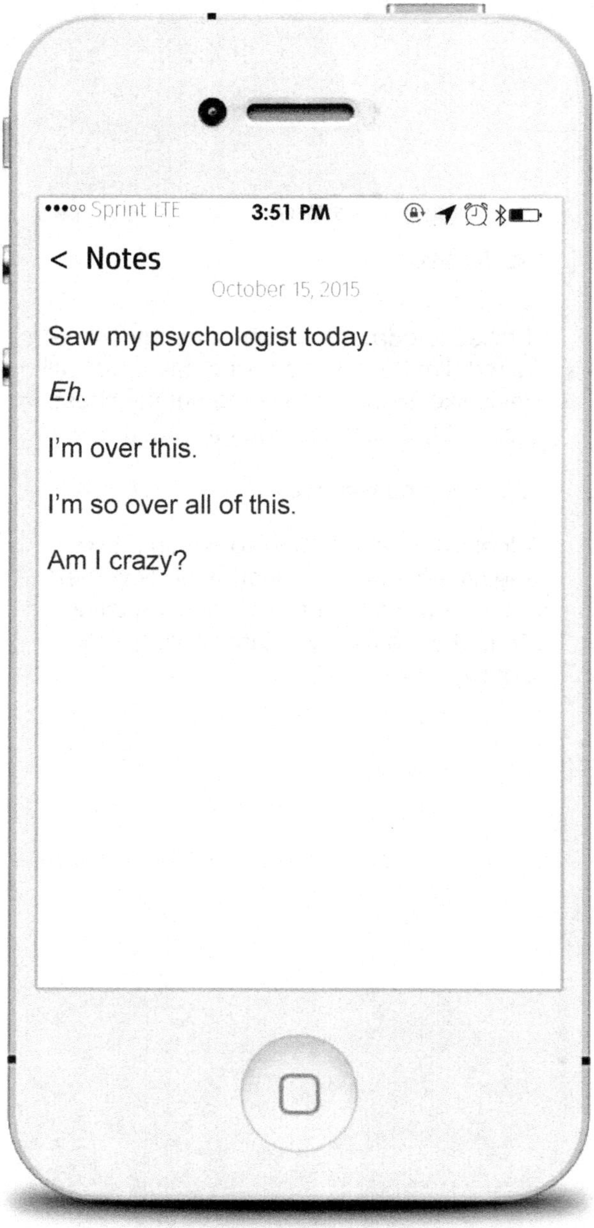
Sprint LTE
3:51 PM
< Notes
October 15, 2015
Saw my psychologist today.
Eh.
I'm over this.
I'm so over all of this.
Am I crazy?

•••○○ Sprint LTE 5:05 AM

< **Notes**

October 20, 2015

I just finished drinking wine and moderating a conversation for one of my best friends and her boo. They have had some rough patches in their relationship over the past few years and are willingly trying to figure out how to make this work, or end it. I hope I helped.

Even in the slightest bit.

Today wasn't about me, and I loved it! The idea of counseling intrigues me and I got a lot of energy from it.

Granted, we all didn't come to a finite conclusion on their next steps, but at least I was able to open a dialogue and get them to actually HEAR each other's grievances. I feel good about this! Hopefully, in the morning, things work themselves out between them.

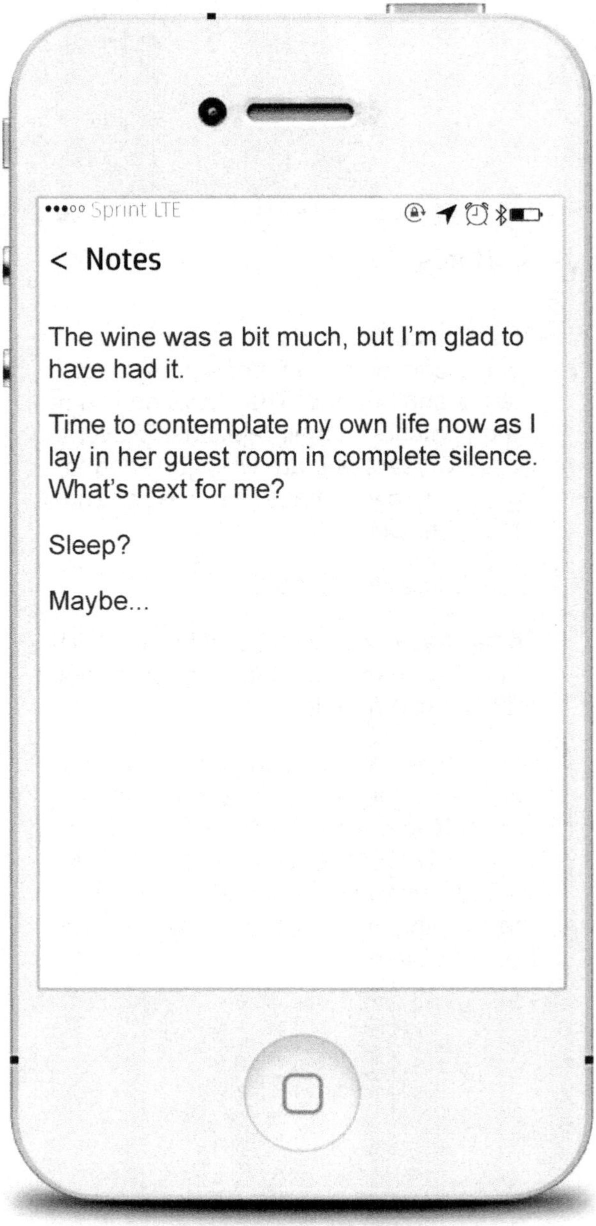
●●●○○ Sprint LTE
< Notes
The wine was a bit much, but I'm glad to have had it.
Time to contemplate my own life now as I lay in her guest room in complete silence. What's next for me?
Sleep?
Maybe...

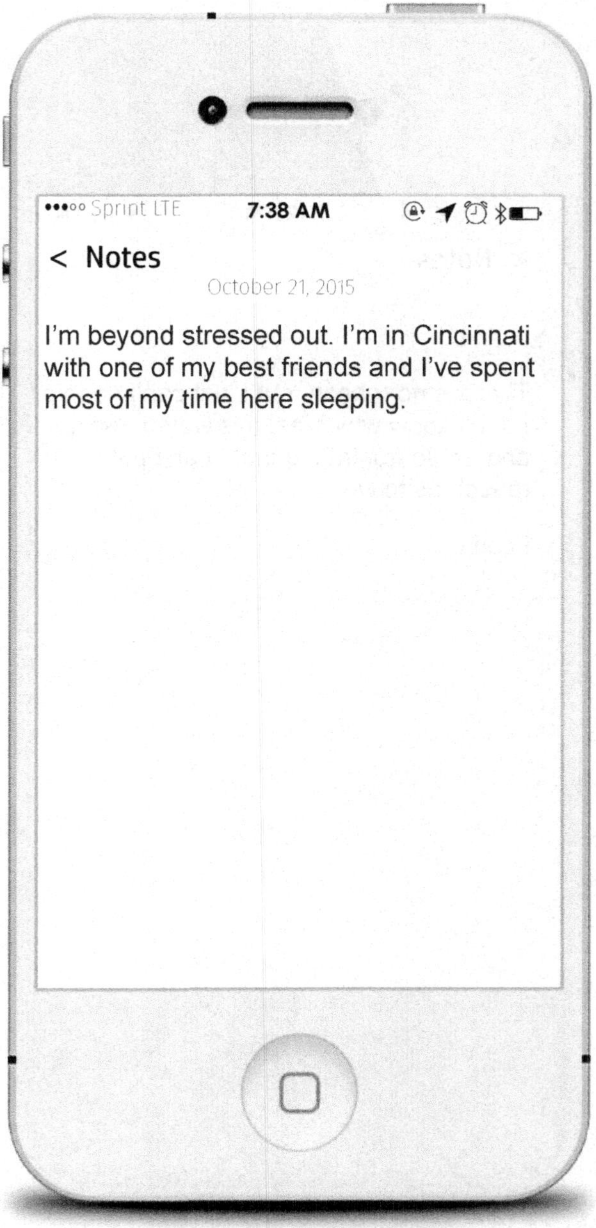
Sprint LTE
7:38 AM
< Notes
October 21, 2015
I'm beyond stressed out. I'm in Cincinnati with one of my best friends and I've spent most of my time here sleeping.

•••○○ Sprint LTE
9:12 AM
< Notes
October 31, 2015
I can't.
There is no reason, but I just can't do this. I don't know why I feel this way- I just do and it's so frustrating that I can't put a reason as to why.
I can't.

•••○○ Sprint LTE 8:08 AM

< Notes

November 1, 2015

What. Is. Wrong. With. Me?

I know people who would do anything to live my life. I mean, why not? I don't work particularly hard, I get to lay in bed all day, play on my phone and talk to my friends if I choose. I can come and go as I please, I don't have any life altering responsibilities…

But I can't enjoy it.

A life of leisure (for lack of a better word), but I would rather pull my hair out or think about cutting myself. I don't get it. I just don't understand.

I thought the pills were supposed to work gradually and help me, it just seems like I'm going backwards.

•••oo Sprint LTE

< Notes

How can I figure out what is wrong with me? Therapy *was* cool, but now I'm left to fend for myself. I can't handle this. I'm going crazy and I just want it all to stop.

But how?

I need a psychoanalyst/psychotherapist on top of the psychiatrist.

•••○○ Sprint LTE
6:08 PM
< Notes
November 2, 2015
Never good enough.

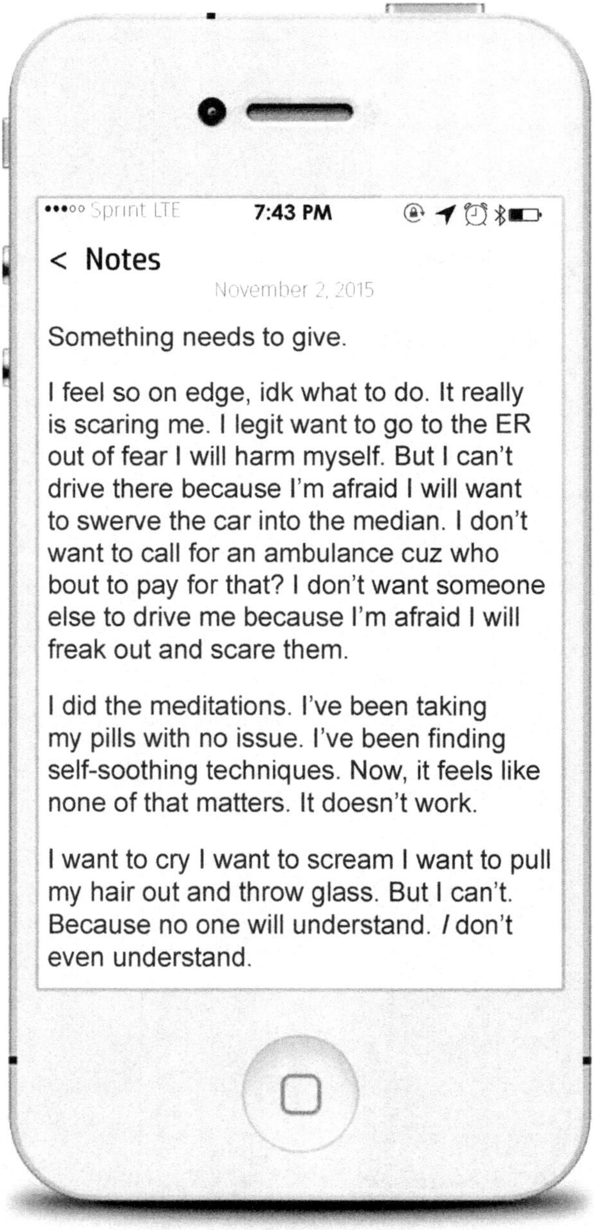
●●●○○ Sprint LTE
7:43 PM
< Notes
November 2, 2015
Something needs to give.
I feel so on edge, idk what to do. It really is scaring me. I legit want to go to the ER out of fear I will harm myself. But I can't drive there because I'm afraid I will want to swerve the car into the median. I don't want to call for an ambulance cuz who bout to pay for that? I don't want someone else to drive me because I'm afraid I will freak out and scare them.
I did the meditations. I've been taking my pills with no issue. I've been finding self-soothing techniques. Now, it feels like none of that matters. It doesn't work.
I want to cry I want to scream I want to pull my hair out and throw glass. But I can't. Because no one will understand. *I* don't even understand.

•••oo Sprint LTE

< Notes

You know how you feel when someone makes you so upset to the point it makes you frustrated and you start crying? It's how I assume girls would feel when they are about to get into a fight in school...

Shaking leg, body hot, hands clenched, tense mouth, *"oooo... I just want to punch her in the face"* type of feeling. The problem for me is, there's no other person. I want to punch *myself* in the face. Quite literally.

It's like I'm spiraling but I know exactly where I'm headed because I've read about this, I've studied it for class, I've learned about it thru theories... It's not a good place. But I don't want to admit it. I don't want to face it. I don't want to accept it.

We'll see.

Sprint LTE
< Notes
Meditation time...

•••oo Sprint LTE 10:03 PM

< Notes

November 2, 2015

11/2/15 10:03pm

Wine.

Because everybody needs moscato.

Most of a bottle, at that.

Honestly, idk how I feel.

Numb.

But tipsy drunk.

Shout out to autocorrect cuz you don't even want to know what this entry originally said.

●●●○○ Sprint LTE
7:20 AM
< Notes
November 4, 2015
Yesterday was a good day.
Today already feels crappy and I literally just woke up.
Sigh.

Sprint LTE
12:59 PM
< Notes
November 4, 2015
When you can't define what is wrong with you it drives you crazy.
...quite literally.

•••oo Sprint LTE 12:01 AM

< Notes

November 5, 2015

I get thee slightest bit stressed and I end up freaking out. I had a deadline to meet by 6pm on the 4th, totally couldn't do it. I made it known that I needed more time, and was granted the extension with no issue.

Here I am at midnight driving myself crazy for not being proactive and starting the project a month ago.

Drea.

It doesn't matter.

You are here now and you have more time, take a breath and get some rest.

Seems logical and easy enough. But, it isn't so easy. I'm getting worked up about my work ethic and being lazy and incapa-

•••oo Sprint LTE

< Notes

ble… I'm questioning my abilities and if I bit off more than I could chew with this.

Why stress? I simply don't understand.

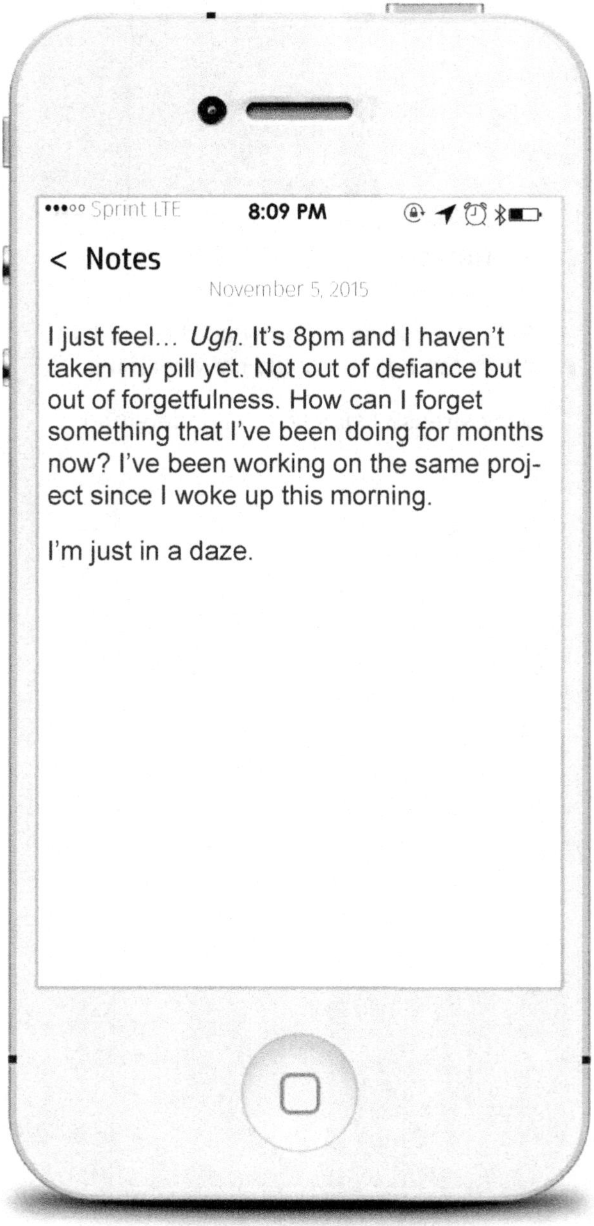
•••oo Sprint LTE
8:09 PM
< Notes
November 5, 2015
I just feel… *Ugh*. It's 8pm and I haven't taken my pill yet. Not out of defiance but out of forgetfulness. How can I forget something that I've been doing for months now? I've been working on the same project since I woke up this morning.
I'm just in a daze.

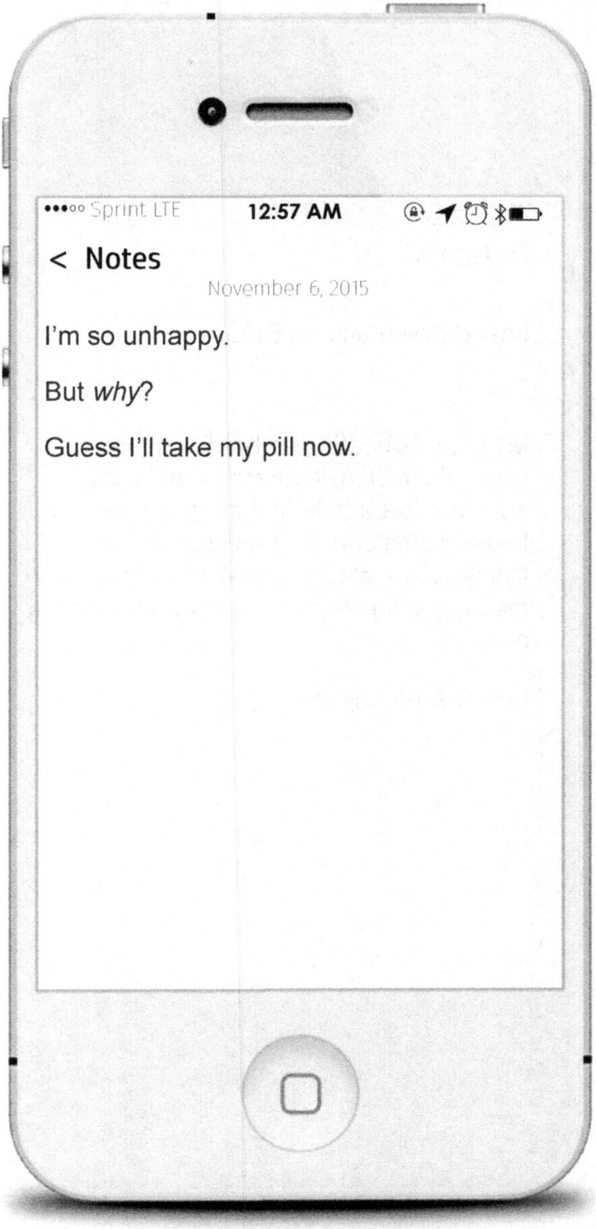
•••oo Sprint LTE
12:57 AM
< Notes
November 6, 2015
I'm so unhappy.
But *why*?
Guess I'll take my pill now.

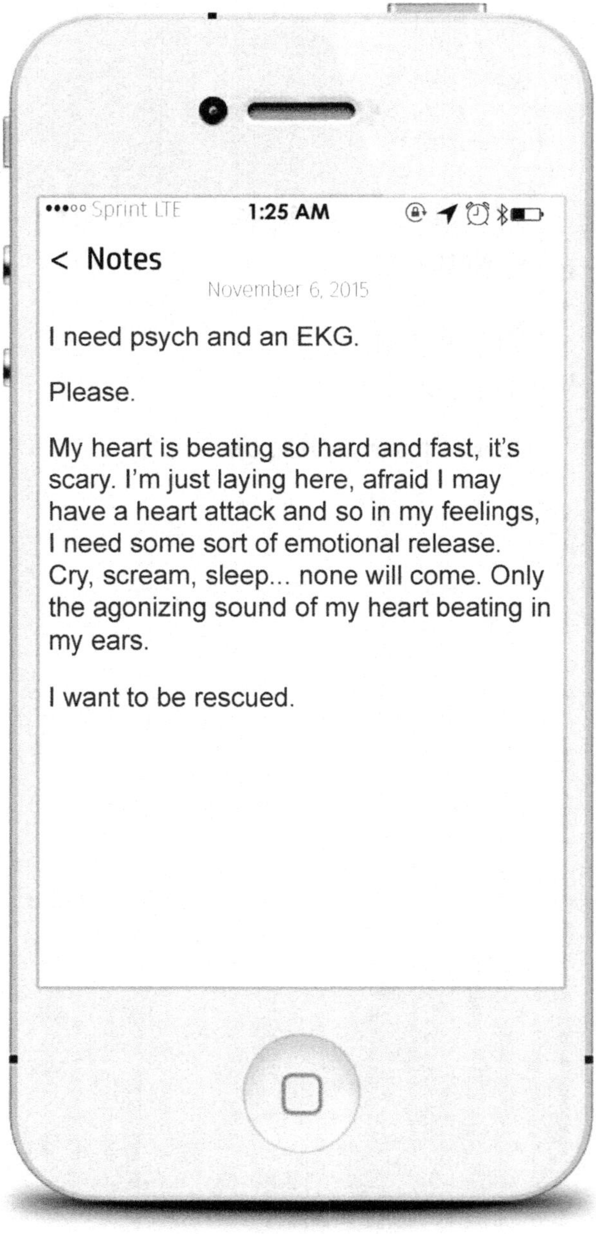
Sprint LTE
1:25 AM
< Notes
November 6, 2015
I need psych and an EKG.
Please.
My heart is beating so hard and fast, it's scary. I'm just laying here, afraid I may have a heart attack and so in my feelings, I need some sort of emotional release. Cry, scream, sleep... none will come. Only the agonizing sound of my heart beating in my ears.
I want to be rescued.

•••○○ Sprint LTE 1:27 AM

< Notes

November 6, 2015

I feel like bouncing off the walls. I'm irritated. I'm frustrated. My head is spinning with a million things yet it feels so empty. I keep telling myself that I am being ungrateful but I. Can't. Help. It.

I want to scream out curse words and cry but I have no desire to cry. Im perfectly fine. I want a hug. I want to feel drunk. I want to laugh. I want to have sex. I'm upset. I'm tired. I'm wide awake. My heart is racing. My breathing feels slow but shallow.

It's too much. Why do I feel like this? I don't like this. Make it stop.

I don't understand. I don't want to feel like this. Something needs to change asap.

I'm really worried.

•••○○ Sprint LTE
< Notes
No…
I'm actually *scared*.

< Notes

November 7, 2015

Wide awake. But for once, my mind is silent.

It's always quiet before the storm.

•••○○ Sprint LTE 8:55 PM

< Notes

November 7, 2015

Today was a seemingly good day. At least, for the most part. I got out the house and took a drive this morning, had a sausage mcmuffin from McDonald's, came home with a splitting headache, slept, finished the project I was working on, drank some water, and now I'm sitting on my bed trying to contemplate my next move in life.

Maybe I want to go to school... Which school?

Maybe I want to work... Who will hire me and pay me a salary?

Maybe I want to move... Where will I go?

It's time (while I'm semi-sane) to make decisions and plans for myself. It's Nove-meber. I'm 27. The year is almost over and I have nothing to show for my accom-

•••○○ Sprint LTE

< Notes

plishments.

It's time to change this. If you want things to be different, you have to do different things.

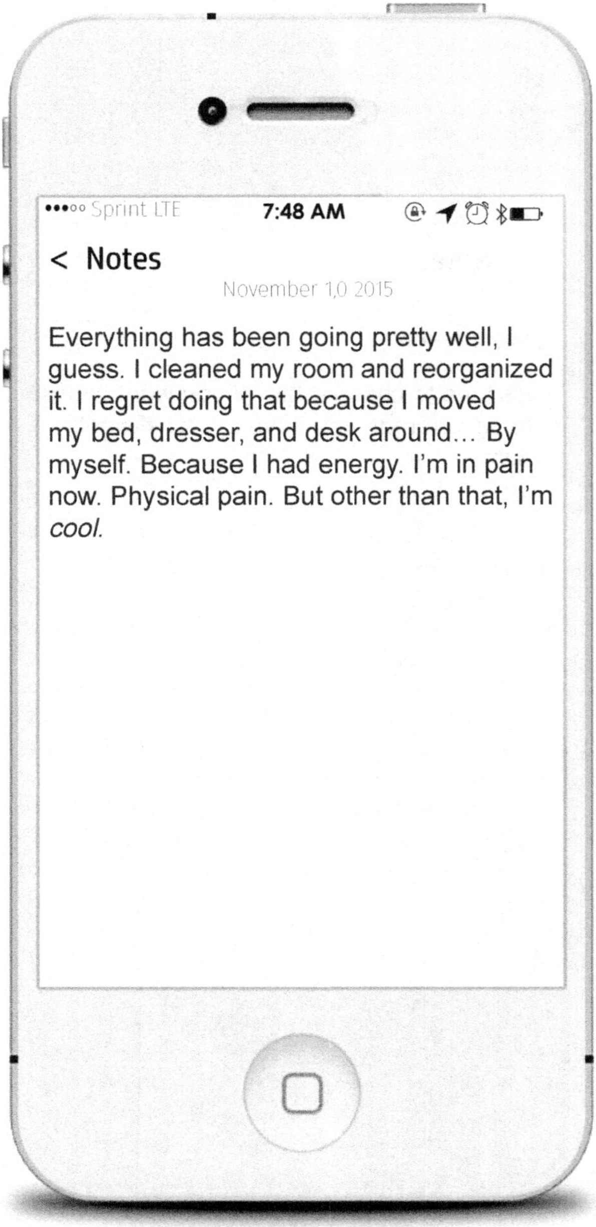

•••oo Sprint LTE
7:48 AM
< Notes
November 1,0 2015
Everything has been going pretty well, I guess. I cleaned my room and reorganized it. I regret doing that because I moved my bed, dresser, and desk around… By myself. Because I had energy. I'm in pain now. Physical pain. But other than that, I'm *cool.*

•••○○ Sprint LTE 3:08 PM

< **Notes**

November 10, 2015

I don't even know how I feel right now.

Just *Blah*.

I've been asleep all day. Now, I just want to stuff my face with pizza and chicken wings from Hooters.

I'm so fat.

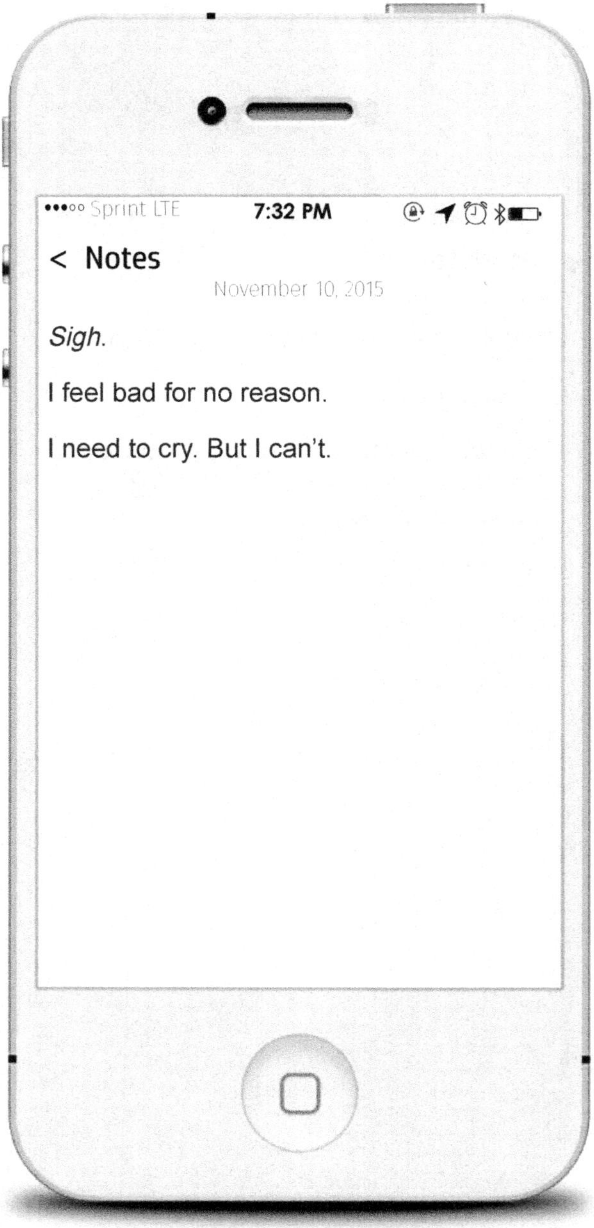
•••oo Sprint LTE
7:32 PM
< Notes
November 10, 2015
Sigh.
I feel bad for no reason.
I need to cry. But I can't.

●●●○○ Sprint LTE
5:30 AM
< Notes
November 11, 2015
I don’t want to be redundant, but…
I’m trying. I really am.
I don’t know what else to do.

Sprint LTE
9:53 AM
< Notes
November 12, 2015
Last counseling session today. I'm not sure how I feel about it yet.

•••oo Sprint LTE 9:06 PM

< **Notes**

November 13, 2015

Story time.

I've always wanted to wake up to a view of the city at sunrise…

Who would have thought it would be like this?

I went to my last psychologist session yesterday. The plan was to figure out next steps in my treatment plan and try to put together some options. While that was definitely on the agenda, I just had to tell her about how I was feeling last week…

open can of worms here

While I explained in detail how I *felt*, I could see her wheels turning. Her mind and attention shifted from being present with me- like she normally is- to trying to

••••○ Sprint LTE

< Notes

figure something out. I mean, she's the professional and I trust her decisions and suggestions as a person of authority, so I didn't argue when she said she wanted to send me to the hospital. At that exact moment.

I questioned how necessary it was since I was feeling *fine*, but she insisted. I willingly signed the release forms, then, I was whisked away in a police car with the director of counseling to the hospital.

When "they" say they're taking you to the ER, it's normal to think of the place you go if you walked in the hospital yourself and you have to sign in with registration and have a seat in the waiting room.

This was not my experience.

•••oo Sprint LTE

< Notes

This lady took me through the *back entrance*. And it was exactly how it sounds.

The back entrance of a large, Trauma 1, urban, community, teaching hospital is not somewhere you want to go if you regularly drink starbucks and order using “starbucks language” fluently. (Triple grande soy vanilla latte extra hot extra foam, anyone?) There were patients there in handcuffs being escorted by police officers. There were patients on stretchers screaming for their lives. This wasn't *Grey's Anatomy*, even on a trauma day. If you want to get into the medical field in a densely populated urban area like Atlanta, trust me, they must either pay you substantially well or you absolutely have to have a deep, deep, *deep* passion for servicing the underserved. It was dark and dismal. There was nowhere

Sprint LTE

< Notes

to stand and wait, cuz obvi, there are no chairs; there is no waiting room. It just is.

If hadn't been there with the counseling director, I for certain, would have turned right back around and walked out. There was no way...

Then, a moment of ER familiarity. Triage.

The triage nurse introduced herself and started taking my vitals. She didn't seem to fit in with the personality of this intense hospital. She spoke softly and didn't have a rushed temperament. It was a pleasant surprise. She then got me a stretcher and once again I was whisked away. This time to psych triage.

If you never have to witness or experience a psych waiting room, of sorts, don't.

•••○○ Sprint LTE

< Notes

It's not pleasant. Especially if you drink starbucks and get upset at your barista for spelling your name on your cup wrong or if you can't use your mobile gift card because you're at a licensed location and not a full-service one. (Target and Barnes & Noble locations come to mind.) As a "perfectly sane" person in that environment, you may actually freak out. There's the guy who had to be restrained, inverted, and sedated because he was yelling for his life and was trying really hard to break out of the stretcher to attack the hospital staff. Then there was the lady who tried to have a conversation with me about the 3rd floor where they cut out organs and sell them... She knows because they did it to her. Oh. The gentleman who thought it was appropriate to expose himself to every passing staff member because he needed

•••○○ Sprint LTE

< Notes

his catheter and folly bag changed... No words. Just flashing.

Again, if you want to go into psych health-care in this setting, make sure it's what you REALLY want to do or that you remain distant and cold towards your patients because you're only there because you get paid 6+ figures.

After changing into a gown and observing my new surroundings, I had my blood drawn and vitals retaken. I met with so many members of the psychiatry team it was unreal. A few residents, an attending, a clinician, the mental health tech, 2 nurses, police officers and security guards. It was too much for me. But I had so much energy, I openly spoke with them and recited my answers to their redundant

•••oo Sprint LTE

< Notes

questions with ease.

THAT was the red flag.

There I was, a relatively young, educated, black girl in this strange place with strange people and I didn't seem distressed. Instead , to them, I was manic.

And just like that, I was again, whisked away. This time to the crisis intervention psych unit. Every movie, TV show, book you have ever seen or read that featured some semblance of a psychiatric hospital or ward was pretty accurately depicted. I won't go into detail here simply because of the laws of the land and out of respect for my fellow patients. Just know that it was a very intense setting to be in and then to have to stay overnight... I had everything taken away... Down to my hair scrunchi. I

•••oo Sprint LTE

< Notes

had absolutely nothing on my body at that point that was mine.

If the medicine doesn't "make me better" then the experience of being hospitalized will. It was just too much...

At least I got to watch the new episode of *Grey's Anatomy*.

Prozac-*lose*

Drea-*win*

Abilify-*CHALLENGER*

•••oo Sprint LTE 6:59 AM

< Notes

November 21, 2015

It's been a few days, to say the least... I have been taking the Abilify just as religiously as I did Zach. The only thing I hate about Billy (my nickname for abilify), is that it makes me sleepy. Like, beyond sleepy. Like, it knocks me out almost immediately.

Bright side...

It allows me to sleep through the night and not *really* need a nap during the day. This allows me to have productive, full days.

Down side...

I have nothing to do during the day, so my energy levels are through the roof. I literally, roll around in my bed everyday, frustrated I can't release the energy. I just need to find something to do to keep me occupied and to exercise.

••••○ Sprint LTE

< Notes

I've been eating more. That's one thing I miss Zach for; my lack of appitite and losing weight. I'm at a good place with my body and it would really suck if I negated all that time and my now-positive-feelings towards myself by eating too much.

But can you really "eat too much" after barely eating at all and losing 15 pounds in the process?

Le sigh.

Here I go again with my negative over-thinking. Why can't I just *be*?

Honestly. I feel like I'm in a waaaay better place than I was a couple weeks ago. I just *feel* better. Maybe I *am* better?

I don't know...

•••○○ Sprint LTE

< Notes

But I'd drink to that if I wasn't so afraid to drink wine. None the less, it is something to celebrate. Hopefully this relationship goes better than Zach's.

Here's to a new beginning with Billy.

Abilify- 6

Drea- 1

Epilogue

Experiencing depression is like experiencing the death of yourself. It is an out of body experience that is hard to explain. You, literally, watch yourself become a shell that cannot function appropriately. It's hard to get out of bed, it's hard to interact with people, it's hard to enjoy the things you once enjoyed...

I get it.

It's *hard.*

One thing people always say to me when I share my feelings is that "everyone feels this way at some point." No. "Everyone" does not feel the same way I do. With depression- and mental illness, in general, you are unable to manage, or regulate how you feel or how you think. Do not mistake me, you can definitely overcome your illness with the proper help and treatment, but when you are suffering in the moment, your feelings are valid; your thoughts are valid. Everything seems so real and you can't help but to succumb to what you are feeling.

There is good news though: There is a light at the end of the tunnel!

For me, I apparently was misdiagnosed and had been on the wrong medication. It was scary that I hadn't made as much progress as I knew I should have made in all that time. Once I had a proper diagnosis and the proper treatment to complement it, everything turned around.

There were way more up days and I was more alert to my environment- not just was happening inside my head.

I want you to know that if you are dealing with mental illness that you can overcome it. Find doctors and therapists you trust and can confide in easily. One thing I learned during this journey is that if I wasn't open and receptive to my psychologist, I wouldn't have had the intervention I did. That last encounter changed my life. If I hadn't been open to her suggestion to been seen at the hospital, I would have went pretending like everything was okay, knowing that something was definitely wrong.

You can get past this. You are strong enough to ask for help when you need it. You are worth overcoming your depression. I've made it this far and so can you . You can make it further than I can if you just believe that you can and put the proper supports in place to get you to where you want to be.

You can do it. I believe in you.

Signed,
The Black Girl on Prozac

Made in United States
North Haven, CT
22 March 2024

50313820R00078